OUT OF THE SHADOWS

OUT OF THE SHADOWS
Essays on 18th & 19th century women

NAOMI CLIFFORD

Copyright © Naomi Clifford 2022
978-1-9196232-9-0

The right of Naomi Clifford to be identified as the author of this work has been asserted by him in accordance with the Copyright, Designs and Patents Act, 1988.

A CIP record for this book is available from the British Library.

All rights reserved. No part of this book may be reproduced or transmitted in any form or by any means, electronic or mechanical including photocopying, recording, or by any information storage and retrieval system, without permission from the Publisher in writing.

Caret Press
9 Durand Gardens, London SW9 0PS
info@caretpress.com   caretpress.com

NAOMI CLIFFORD is an acclaimed author and history writer. She is a host of The Door history podcast, co-editor of Vauxhall History website and chairman of Friends of Stockwell War Memorial and Gardens.

She was born in London into an American family and has been a committed historian since the age of eight, when a 'Jackdaw' folder of reproduced original documents about the slave trade fired up her imagination. She studied history at Bristol University and, after a career in magazines, returned to her first love, history, especially the history of women on the margins.

Her published works include *The Disappearance of Maria Glenn* (2016), which looks at the fate of a young girl who was abducted in 1817 from her home in Taunton; *Women and the Gallows 1797-1837: Unfortunate Wretches*, an exploration of the stories of women hanged in England and Wales; *The Murder of Mary Ashford*, which recounts the case of a young woman whose rape and murder in Birmingham still excites controversy. Naomi Clifford's latest book, *Under Fire* (2021), which uses the diaries of a volunteer ambulance driver to tell the story of the London Blitz, has been praised as 'one of the best descriptive accounts of the World War Two bombing of Chelsea and London.'

NAOMI CLIFFORD is an acclaimed author and history writer. She is a host of The Door history podcast, co-editor of Vauxhall History website and chairman of Friends of Stockwell War Memorial and Gardens.

She was born in London into an American family and has been a committed historian since the age of eight, when a 'Jackdaw' folder of reproduced original documents about the slave trade fired up her imagination. She studied history at Bristol University and, after a career in magazines, returned to her first love, history, especially the history of women on the margins.

Her published works include *The Disappearance of Maria Glenn* (2016), which looks at the fate of a young girl who was abducted in 1817 from her home in Taunton; *Women and the Gallows 1797-1837: Unfortunate Wretches*, an exploration of the stories of women hanged in England and Wales; *The Murder of Mary Ashford*, which recounts the case of a young woman whose rape and murder in Birmingham still excites controversy. Naomi Clifford's latest book, *Under Fire* (2021), which uses the diaries of a volunteer ambulance driver to tell the story of the London Blitz, has been praised as 'one of the best descriptive accounts of the World War Two bombing of Chelsea and London.'

OUT OF THE SHADOWS

	Introduction	*viii*
1	'I am murdered': The death of Eliza Fenning	2
2	Love & lies in the age of elopement	32
3	Mrs Meredith, the prisoners' friend	44
4	The abolition of the jury of matrons	56
5	Cartes de visite of working women	72
6	Trial by Battle: The opening night of the Royal Coburg	88
7	The communard and anarchist Louise Michel in Lambeth	100

INTRODUCTION

I HAVE TITLED this slender volume of essays *Out of the Shadows* because it features women whose stories, in one way or another, have either not had the exposure they deserve or have had none at all. Women's history and women's histories are often, even now, consigned to the sidelines, ghettoised in bookshops and libraries as a 'special interest', as if the protagonists were spectators in the arena of history rather than actors. Perhaps my efforts can be seen as a small contribution to the wider aim of bringing women's lives centre stage.

As individuals, some of the women in these pages will be well known to you. I have tried to explore new dimensions of their lives. The socialist and anarchist Louise Michel is certainly famous enough, especially in Europe, but perhaps her fact-finding visit to Lambeth in south London in 1883 is not. Mary Ashford's murder in 1817 is remembered in Birmingham more than two hundred years after her death–indeed, I wrote a book about it–but the allied events on the stage of the Royal Coburg theatre on its opening night are less so.

Many of the more obscure women in the essays would have remained in perpetual shadow but for some catastrophic circumstance that brought them to the attention of the public. Eliza Fenning, who in all likelihood went to her death innocent of the heinous crime of which she was accused, would not have become a cause célèbre had not the ruling classes been particularly jittery over social unrest and specifically the discontent among their servants. The abducted women in 'Love & lies', who came to my attention when I researched the case of Maria

Glenn, a teenager targeted for her reputed fortune, also would not have found infamy but for the crimes committed against them. These individuals were once the talk of households across the country but they were swiftly forgotten–misogyny, and indeed bride abduction, have not disappeared and it felt right to bring them back into our collective memory. The piece on the jury of matrons explores the rules around the sentencing of pregnant women to death and their astonishingly tardy amendment, a subject made painfully pertinent by recent changes in reproductive rights, particularly in the US.

Most of the essays have emerged from my research for books I have written or am currently writing. Some are the products of my falling into 'rabbit holes' in pursuit of those subjects. They may not have made the final cut but I could not let them go to waste. I have a strong desire to share the treasures I have unearthed.

Nearly all the essays have a darkness of tone, for which I do not apologise. My interest is for the most part in the lower end of the social hierarchy and that often leads to women who were trapped in moral cul-de-sacs. When people are faced with stark choices the consequences often include transgression of some kind. Ultimately, however, the essays address subjects that I simply found interesting. The hope is that you will too.

NAOMI CLIFFORD
July 2022

'I AM MURDERED'
The death of ELIZA FENNING

My aching heart with pity bled,
When poor Eliza! Cloth'd in white;
At Newgate drop't her lovely head,
And clos'd her eyes in endless night.

*From a contemporary broadside
published on the execution of Eliza Fenning*

IN 1806 HENRY WYATT, a fifteen-year-old apprentice watch wheel finisher, appeared at the Old Bailey in London accused of trying to kill his employer and his family by lacing their coffee with arsenic. Henry had drunk some of the coffee and fell ill afterwards and, although a witness established that Henry knew where the arsenic was kept in the household, no one saw him administer it. A motive could not be established. The prosecution failed and Henry was acquitted. Henry's defence lawyer was Peter Alley.[1] Nine years later, Alley defended Eliza Fenning, a young cook-maid charged with trying to kill her employer and his family by sprinkling arsenic on dumplings. The case had remarkable similarities to Wyatt's: Eliza herself had been poisoned, she was said to have known where the arsenic was stored, and no one saw her use it. The jury in her case brought back a guilty verdict, and in July 1815, dressed in white and vehemently protesting her innocence, she

FIG.1 An idealised portrait of Eliza Fenning, published in 1815, after her death.
*From 'Affecting Case of Eliza Fenning, Who Suffered the Sentence of the Law'.
London: John Fairburn*

was hanged in the street outside Newgate. Why, given the weakness of the case against her, was she not acquitted as Henry was?[2]

On 30 January 1815 Eliza Fenning arrived in the Turner household at 68 Chancery Lane to begin a new job. She had been hired by Margaret Turner to work for her daughter-in-law Charlotte, who was married to Margaret's son Robert. Margaret's husband Orlibar owned a law stationery business that operated out of the Chancery Lane address but the Margaret and Orlibar had since moved to Vauxhall on the south side of the Thames, while Robert and Charlotte, who were expecting their first child, lived at Chancery Lane. The household also included a maid, Sarah Peer, and Roger Gadsden and Thomas King, both of them teenaged law stationery apprentices.

At twenty-one Eliza was young, although not much younger than Charlotte herself, and had an excellent character and good experience: she had been in service from the age of fourteen and had already had eight jobs. She was also bright and amusing and could read and write. Her first two weeks went well, when the senior Mr and Mrs Turner stayed at Chancery Lane to help her settle in, but then they returned to Vauxhall, leaving Eliza to be managed by Charlotte.

For Eliza, this position was an opportunity to prove her skills in a solidly middle-class establishment, but it quickly became apparent that it was not without its problems. Charlotte Turner had been married only eight months and was still finding her feet as a mistress. Eliza noticed that she had a habit of closely supervising her, questioning what she was doing and finding fault, and much preferred working for Margaret Turner. There were other tensions too. Sarah Peer, the maid, was cool towards her but seemed to be close with Charlotte. Before long, the two servants fell out when Eliza made the mistake of using one of Sarah's shifts as a duster but, never one to brood, Eliza assumed they had managed to smooth things over. She put her energies into managing the kitchen efficiently.

Feelings between the inhabitants of 68 Chancery Lane came to a head one night in early March. On her journey up to bed Eliza's candle blew out, so she knocked at the apprentices' bedroom door to beg a light. Eliza later described what happened: '[They] began taking liberties I did not approve of.' It is likely that it was Roger Gadsden who was trying to flirt with Eliza as Thomas King suffered from excruciating shyness. 'I told them if they dared to insult me, I would call Mrs Turner, which I did, but she not coming at the instant, I went to my own room and, when nearly undressed, Mrs Turner came into the room and asked me what was the matter, I informed her of what had passed, and she said she did not approve of such behaviour.'

Rather than discipline the apprentices, however, Charlotte criticised Eliza and the next morning told her that if she could not 'behave better' she would have to leave. Eliza came back quickly with a threat of her own:

> If she did not approve of my conduct when my mistress [Margaret Turner] returned I was willing to leave, at which she was so enraged that she sent for her husband [Robert], and he desired me to leave the house, but the same evening my mistress [Margaret Turner] returned, she asked me kindly how I did, and I told her I was going to leave, and stated the facts to her. She then called her daughter[-in-law], and told her I should not leave her house; everything was then settled, and I thought to be comfortable as before. I went on with my business as usual for some time.

The following day, still a little bruised by the injustice of Charlotte Turner's accusation, Eliza told Sarah Peer that she no longer liked her mistress.

This minor conflict, which later formed the motive for Eliza's alleged murderous plot, illustrates perfectly Eliza's personality: confident, assertive and unwilling to subordinate herself, even to her social superiors. She knew she was in the right and that she had been unjustly accused. Perhaps her attitude should not surprise us: her family was poor but it was stable and loving, and she was well educated for a young woman of her rank. Until she was twelve, Eliza attended Gate Street Charity School in Lincoln's Inn Fields, which was run by Dissenters, and at fourteen entered service. She was a good-looking young woman and naturally attracted admirers, and by 1815 she had committed to a young man called Edward (whose surname is unknown) and hoped to marry him. Generally, she was seen as good company: personable, friendly and witty. Only one of her former employers, Mr Hardy, a grocer in Portugal Street, had cause for complaint; after her death he said she was 'a hoity-toity, wild, giddy, unsettled sort of girl, curious and inquisitive, and minding what did not concern her.' He strongly disapproved of her habit of reading books.

FIG.2 Riots were endemic in London, especially over food issues. The presentation of a new Corn Bill provoked disturbances outside the house of its sponsor, Frederick John Robinson. *'A London Riot' by Charles Reuben Ryley (1752–1798), undated; pen and black ink and wash. Courtesy of Yale Center for British Art, Paul Mellon Collection, B1977.14.5130*

Eliza's father, William Fenning, had been a bandsman with the 15th Regiment of Foot, having joined the army as a young man to escape a life as an agricultural labourer in his native Suffolk. He was sent to Ireland, where he met and in 1790 married Mary Swayne, a Protestant, the daughter of a slater and granddaughter of a London silversmith. A subsequent posting took the couple to Dominica in the West Indies, where they started a family. Mary gave birth to ten children, of whom Eliza, born on the island in 1793, was the cherished only survivor.

William Fenning left the army in 1802 and the family returned to England, eventually settling in London where he worked as a labourer for his brother, a potato dealer, and Mary found employment as an upholsterer. In early 1815, after the apparent end of the wars with France, William perhaps would have had sympathy with the unemployed soldiers trickling back into England, and especially into London, who were blamed for a spike in crime. According to the government's figures, the number of committals had leapt twenty-five per cent between 1814 and 1815 after a dip of ten per cent the previous year. The middle classes trembled and muttered. Newspapers reported that 'the increase of crimes in the capital is truly alarming'.

During the years of war, France's blockade had prevented foreign grain imports reaching Britain. The rich had grown richer by selling wheat and other grains at a premium and they were not about to allow this to change. The poor, already pushed to breaking point, feared they would starve. In February Member of Parliament Frederick John Robinson announced that he would bring in a new Corn Law to forbid the import of cheap foreign wheat until the price at home reached eighty shillings (£4) a bushel. Protest was immediate, from farmers, who felt protection did not go far enough, and from the poor, who complained that it kept the price of bread artificially high. When Robinson presented his bill on 7 March, a mob gathered in the streets around the Palace of Westminster with the aim of stopping MPs from entering the House. The protesters were unsuccessful, and afterwards moved on to the homes of supporters of the bill, breaking windows and pulling down iron railings to turn them into weapons.

Outside Robinson's residence in Old Burlington Street, Edward Vyse, a nineteen-year-old midshipman who was minding his own business and had no part in the disturbances, was shot and killed by someone firing from inside the house. William Hone, a radical defender of press freedom and persistent thorn in the side of the government, disgusted by this callous disregard for life, took up the search for the truth of what had happened. He denounced as unconstitutional the coroner's attempts to manipulate the jury's verdict of wilful murder. Later Hone would turn his attention to Eliza's fate.

DESPITE THE ROW over her 'indelicate' behaviour, Eliza was generally content at Chancery Lane. She went to market to buy provisions and argued about prices and quality with the butcher and the baker. In the kitchen, she made soups, pies and suet puddings, prepared vegetables and joints for boiling or roasting for Robert and Charlotte Turner, and for Margaret and Orlibar Turner when they visited. As was usual practice, she also cooked separate, cheaper meals for herself, Sarah and the apprentices. She learned to work around Charlotte Turner's watchfulness.

On Saturday 18 March, when the brewer's man delivered some beer for Robert Turner, Eliza asked him for some yeast. On Monday he dropped it off with Sarah, who put it in a basin ready for Eliza to use later that day to make dumplings. Eliza described what happened the following day, Tuesday 21 March:

> I went up for orders for dinner, as usual; my mistress asked me what there was in the house, I told her that the brewer had brought some yeast, at which she seemed pleased… she told me she should have some beef steaks and potatoes for dinner, and dumplings; and to have a meat pie for the kitchen [for the servants and apprentices].[3]

Charlotte Turner said later that she made it clear that she preferred Eliza to use baker's dough for the dumplings and that Eliza campaigned hard to be allowed to make the dough herself from scratch, much to Charlotte's annoyance. Eliza said that this was not true: there had been no such insistence.

> I went down and made the pie and had everything in readiness for making the dumplings; when she [Charlotte] came into the kitchen she told me to take the pie to the oven and then to make the dumplings, but to be sure not to leave the kitchen after the dumplings were made.

At some point that morning, Eliza was interrupted by the delivery of coal to the house. She then made the dough with flour, water, salt and yeast, covered it with a cloth and set it to rise by the fire.

> Then I was sent to the butcher's, for the steaks, when I came back I went into the back-kitchen to clean a dozen and a half knives and forks; during the time I was doing them I heard some person in the front kitchen, and thought it was my mistress, but, on my coming out of the back-kitchen, I saw Thomas King, one of the apprentices, coming out: I asked him what he had been doing in the kitchen, he made no answer, and went upstairs.

Charlotte Turner came down at about half past two and sent Sarah Peer for some milk. She wanted to make the sauce for the dumplings herself. After the dumplings had been boiled, Sarah took them upstairs. Then she went to Hackney, north of London, for the afternoon, to see her sister. Eliza took the steaks and potatoes up to the Turners' table and brought the uneaten dumplings back down to the kitchen. She ate almost all of one of them.

> ...when Gadsden, one of the apprentices, came down and asked me to give him some dumpling; I told him they were cold and heavy, but I gave him a piece and some of the sauce; he then left the kitchen.

Ten minutes later, Robert Turner arrived in the kitchen and said he was ill, and so were his wife and father. They were retching, vomiting and in pain. Now Eliza herself began to feel ill ('violent sick, and an uncommon pain in my head'). At half past three Robert Turner told her he was sure she had put poison in the dumplings but that he thought it was accidental. Gadsden had only eaten a small amount of the dumpling and felt nauseous but had not thrown up, so he was dispatched to fetch Henry Ogilvy, an apothecary and friend of the family, who lived a few doors away. That evening at about eight, Thomas King, who had not eaten any of the dumplings, was sent to fetch John Marshall, a surgeon living in Piccadilly who had known the family for a decade. Marshall later described finding Eliza on the stairs 'apparently in great agony, and complaining of a burning pain in the stomach, with violent reaching [retching], head-ach [sic], and great thirst.' He told her to drink milk and water and then proceeded upstairs to attend to the

Turners. He treated Robert with laudanum and hot flannels to alleviate his agonising stomach pain; he had serious fears that Charlotte would lose her baby (she was now seven months pregnant). Orlibar also had symptoms but they were not as severe as his son and daughter-in-law's. At various points in the night Marshall prescribed sugar water with milk and a dose of castor oil, Epsom salts, mint, saline solution and soda water, remedies he later claimed led to the family's salvation.

Despite her illness, Eliza managed to get a note to her father's place of work near Red Lion Court, asking him to come to the house. He arrived between nine and ten, the message having earlier slipped his mind, only to be refused at the door. Sarah, on Charlotte's orders, lied to him and said that Eliza was out on an errand.

There were, of course, many instances of genuinely warm, familial attachments between servants and their employers but, possibly more commonly, servants and employers lived together out of necessity rather than affection. The relationship was a fine balance. The middle-classes were obsessed with their servants and constantly discussed their shortcomings, betrayals, laziness, suspicious behaviour and sullenness. What were they really thinking while going through the motions of subservience and obedience? Were they hiding a seething hatred of their masters and mistresses?

A few high-profile cases gave employers real cause for concern and seemed to justify their wariness. No one was immune. The Duke of Cumberland's valet had attacked him one night in 1810, and then slit his own throat in his room (that was the story given to the public—the truth may have been more complicated). Three years before the Turners were poisoned, the Count and Countess d'Antraigues, French *emigrés* living in Barnes, a suburb on the western outskirts of London, were murdered by their mentally unhinged Italian servant. And everyone knew cases in which servants, out of 'envy', thieved and filched from their employers or invited their friends into the house to rob them after dark.

However, if there was anything the middle class feared and loathed more than a disloyal servant, it was one with access to arsenic.

In between his ministrations to the victims, John Marshall inspected the dishes in the kitchen. When he saw white particles thickly distributed on the surface of the remaining dumplings in the pan he decided to do some scientific experiments. First he cut a

FIG.3 William Hone, Radical and thorn in the side of the government.
From F.W. Hackford (1912), William Hone: His Life and Times. London: R.D. Unwin. Courtesy of University of California Libraries

small piece of the dumpling into thin slices, put one on a halfpenny balanced on the blade of a knife and held it over the flame of a candle. He detected a garlic smell. When the coin cooled, it was covered in 'silvery whiteness, occasioned by the fumes of the arsenic'. Marshall then examined the knives the family had used at dinner and found them 'deeply tarnished'. That tipped the balance. He was convinced that the family had been poisoned with arsenic and that Eliza was responsible.

In Marshall's eyes, everything Eliza did was suspect. Despite being in great pain, she had refused to take any of the potions he and Ogilvy offered, declaring that 'she had much rather die than live, as life was of no consequence to her', although she eventually gave in and took them or appeared to do so (Margaret Turner informed Marshall the next day that she had not taken any of them). Marshall interpreted this behaviour as extreme remorse at her unsuccessful attempt to kill the Turners, which had caused her to become suicidal.

By the next day, Wednesday, all the victims had improved but were still bedridden, including Eliza, who was arguably the worst affected. Marshall continued his scientific proofs by looking at the earthen dish in which the dumplings had been kneaded. After scraping it out, he diluted the dough, poured in water, stirred briskly and allowed it to settle. He claimed to have retrieved 'full half a teaspoonful of white arsenic'. He heated some of it between copper plates and detected, again, the odour of garlic and observed silvery whiteness on the plates.

On Thursday Orlibar Turner checked the drawer in the office where he had kept scrap paper used as spills to light the fire as well as two packets wrapped up and marked 'Arsenic—Deadly Poison'. One packet was missing and no one could remember seeing it since shortly after Eliza's dispute with Charlotte over the 'indelicate' behaviour.

Orlibar Turner paid a visit to Eliza in her room. Arsenic was missing, he told her, and he was sure it was her doing. Then Margaret Turner arrived to question Eliza.

'What did you put in the dumplings to make us so ill?'

'It was not in the dumplings, but in the milk Sarah Peer brought in.'

Later Eliza wrote, 'When they say I was sure it was in the milk, I really thought so, for milk is a thing that does not agree on my stomach which made me not know which it could be.' Perhaps Eliza's aversion to milk was why she refused Marshall's remedies.

'Did anyone else have a hand in making the dumplings?' asked Mrs Turner.

No, said Eliza. She alone had made them.

THE TURNERS MOVED swiftly against Eliza. Orlibar Turner and John Marshall went to Hatton Garden police office to report the incident and ask for assistance. Officers arrived to search the house. Marshall alleged later that Eliza had tried to dress herself in order to flee but had fainted and that a book containing information about abortion was found among her possessions. After this they took her to be examined by the magistrate at Hatton Garden, where the clerk was a personal friend of the Turners. From there she was transferred to Clerkenwell prison and a police officer was ordered to watch her.

On 25 March the 'diabolical attempt' was reported inaccurately in *The Globe*, which had already decided that Eliza was guilty: 'A female servant in the family of Mr T—r, in the west end of the town, mixed a large quantity of arsenic in a pie.' *The Globe* took up the story again on 27 March, remarking that people could scarcely believe that a servant would poison a whole family and that they 'could not credit it, thinking there could not be such a monster in human nature' but it was the scale of the attack rather than the attack itself, a servant taking revenge on her employer, that was seen as incredible.

Tantalisingly, the report in *The Globe* included this sentence: 'We understand that there is some slight suspicion attached to another person.' In reality, however, once Eliza was accused, and certainly once she was arrested, there was no attempt on the part of her prosecutors to look further into the case. Nothing more appears to have been said on this subject, in print at least, and as the records of the case have been lost or destroyed it is impossible now to identify this other suspect. Despite this, as we shall see, it is possible to speculate that there were at least two other potential perpetrators.

In Clerkenwell prison, Eliza, although still ill, slowly shook off the effects of the poison, but as she did so her mental state deteriorated. She was deeply mortified at her predicament. On Tuesday 29 March she wrote to her 'fiancé' Edward, assuring him that she was innocent and that she expected to be cleared at the next hearing. 'I now lay ill at the infirmary sick ward. My mother attends me three times a day, and brings me everything I can wish for; but, Edward, I never shall be right or happy again, to think I ever was in prison.' On Thursday she appeared before the magistrate again. This time the main witnesses—the Turners, Sarah Peer and Roger Gadsden—gave evidence and she was committed for trial.

Edward did not write back, so Eliza wrote to him again on Friday. It was a comfort that she had his portrait and previous letters with her, she said, but she had heard from her father that he had gone to a party with another woman: 'I am glad to hear that you can spend your time so agreeably with another.' She did not tell him that she was due to be transferred to Newgate prison prior to her trial, which would take place within days. The magistrate had offered her a choice: bail with two sureties of £50 each, a year on remand in Clerkenwell prison, or a swift trial at the current Old Bailey sessions. The Fennings had no funds for bail and Eliza wanted a speedy resolution, so she opted for the Old Bailey.

Forbidding, fortress-like, grim, gloomy, disease-ridden, grey, noisy, stinking: any number of awful adjectives can be used to describe Newgate in 1815. Writing just over twenty years later, Charles Dickens called it the 'gloomy depository of the guilt and misery of London'.[4] When the Quaker prison reformer Elizabeth Fry first visited the wards in 1813 she was almost lost for words: 'The filth, the closeness of the room, the ferocious manners, and the abandoned wickedness which everything bespoke are quite indescribable.' Women were living amid urine and excrement; babies were struggling to breathe the fetid air full of tobacco smoke. It was misery incarnate.

Eliza's parents managed to borrow enough money to pay for a shared cell away from the hell of the wards, and from here she wrote to Edward again. Her trial would be in a week, she said. She had nothing to fear. She was innocent and would soon be cleared. Her parents had borrowed a further five pounds to pay an attorney to draw up a brief for a barrister to plead for her. She continued to hope for Edward's loyalty, but word had reached her that he was friendly with another young woman: 'I am not apt to be jealous, therefore think no more about it; but I firmly believe you are still true and faithful to me; and as you to me, I have fixed my mind and heart entirely on you.' She asked for a line or two, 'if you can spare the time.'

ELIZA WAS TRIED at the Old Bailey on Tuesday 11 April 1815. She was prosecuted by her employer, Orlibar Turner, who was represented in court by John Gurney, and employed as his solicitor the magistrate's clerk who had been at Eliza's examination. Most accused felons were unrepresented, so Eliza was fortunate to have a defence lawyer, Peter Alley, a blunt Irishman known for his experience and all-round competence, but he had been given the brief at the last moment, with no time to prepare. Possibly also he recognised the similarities between Eliza's case and that of the fifteen-year-old watchmaker's apprentice Henry Wyatt, whom he defended almost ten years earlier, and thought this case would be an easy win.

Defence barristers in felony cases were severely restricted in what they could do or say in court. They could not cross-examine, except on facts, nor could they directly address the jury, but the best of them could undermine the prosecution by posing an apposite question on a matter of fact. The famous barrister William Garrow made cross-examination into an art form. Alley, although praised for his skills, was no Garrow and, it seems, he had more important places to be than the Old Bailey.

If Eliza had appeared before almost any other judge, she may have been acquitted or her sentence commuted to transportation or prison. It was her misfortune that John Silvester, the seventy-year-old Recorder of London, heard the case. He had followed a standard route to the bar: Oxford, admission to the Middle Temple, years as a barrister for prosecution and defence, and had accumulated along the way a reputation for slimy lechery and a fondness for the black cap.[5] Contemporary reports on the conduct of the trial still have the power to shock, but the half-truths asserted by the Turners, Roger Gadsden and Sarah Peer and the witnesses' obvious collusion, were nothing compared to the bias of the Recorder.

Charlotte Turner told the court that on the night of the candle incident she had seen Eliza enter the apprentices' room 'partly undressed', which immediately established Eliza in the eyes of the jury as indecent and immoral. She said that Eliza had persistently begged to let her make the dumplings (Eliza said she had spoken to her about them only on the morning she made them), that no one else had access to the kitchen during the morning they were made (wrong on two counts: the coal had been delivered that morning, which Charlotte Turner and Sarah Peer adamantly denied, and Eliza had gone out to buy steak when anyone

FIG.4 Eliza Fenning reading her bible in Newgate prison.
After George Cruikshank, published after her death by William Hone. From F.W. Hackford (1912), William Hone: His Life and Times. London: R.D. Unwin. Courtesy of University of California Libraries

could have been in the kitchen without her knowing), and that the dumplings Eliza served were black and heavy, something she had not noticed enough to mention at the time and which Eliza later said was untrue. Roger Gadsden swore that he had several times seen Eliza open the drawer where the arsenic was kept, in order to get spills to light the fire. John Marshall, the surgeon, told the court that there was no arsenic in the flour tub but it was present in the dumpling dough. He described his scientific experiments and presented them as incontrovertible proof.

Five character witnesses spoke well of Eliza. Her defence was simple: 'I am innocent of the whole charge. I am innocent. Indeed I am! I liked my place. I was very comfortable.' She could not stop herself speaking out in court when Charlotte Turner described Eliza's 'indelicate' behaviour. Later she wrote, 'When I heard Mrs Turner speak falsely of me, being in the boys' bedroom, I contradicted her, knowing it to be false; and when Mr Turner said I never assisted them when they were ill, I was going to speak, but everything seemed in such confusion, that I was not heard to speak, and I not knowing the ways of the trial, I did not know hardly what to say, for everyone's eyes were on me, as if I was the greatest criminal on earth.'

Towards the end of the trial, Eliza pleaded to be allowed to call Thomas King, the shy apprentice, 'for he will not dare to deny the truth. He will say I always asked for paper [to light the fire in the office] when I wanted it.'

'You should have had him here before,' said Silvester.

'My Lord, I desired him to be brought, and wish him to be sent for now.'

'No. It's too late now—I cannot hear you.'

Quite against protocol, Silvester then asked Roger Gadsden whether Eliza ever lit the fire in the office.

'Yes. I and my fellow apprentice have seen her go to that drawer many times.' That he was allowing Gadsden to swear to what another person had seen did not bother Silvester.

During the trial, Eliza's father William had tried to get a note to Silvester to say that his daughter had told him before the poisoning that she liked her place. He had rushed away from court to the Pitt's Head public house opposite the sessions house to write it on a scrap of paper, but was so distressed, his hand shaking so much, that he could not manage it. A friend tried to help, but he could not form the letters either and eventually they asked a stranger to write it. They managed to get it presented to Silvester, but he would not accept it. Instead, he announced, 'It is too late,' and proceeded to sum up. By this stage Peter Alley, Eliza's defence barrister, had left the court on an unknown errand.

Silvester fixed on Eliza's declaration to Sarah Peer that she no longer liked Charlotte Turner, on her alleged repeated requests to make dumplings rather than accept Charlotte's wisdom that the baker's dough was best, and on her warning to Gadsden not to eat the cold leftover dumplings. He pointed out that Eliza would be able to read 'Arsenic — Deadly Poison' on the packets kept in the drawer in the office and that she had not bothered to assist the Turner family when they were struck down. (He did not consider that she herself was poisoned was the reason for this.) Notably, he asserted that 'although we have nothing before us but circumstantial evidence, yet it often happens that circumstances are more conclusive than the most positive testimony'.

The jury conferred and after a few minutes came back with a verdict of guilty. Eliza collapsed screaming and had to be carried out of court. When she was brought back, the Recorder put on his black cap and pronounced sentence of death.

Eliza wrote to Edward that evening: 'They have, which is the cruellest thing in this world, brought me in guilty, because I had the fire to light in the office where the arsenic was kept, and my master said that I went often into the office for things, and so, on that account, they suppose that I must have taken the arsenic out of the drawer, which is the most horrid thing I ever can think of.' She knew the shame of her conviction would be too much for him. It was easier to let him go: 'Pray make your mind happy, and get someone else that will never bring any reflection on you. I shall never think of marrying any person excepting yourself; but I must for ever give up any thought of such, as it may hurt your character; but I still love and respect you.'

TWO DAYS LATER, in the dismal condemned cell at Newgate, Eliza was receiving visitors and fighting despair. After weeks of silence, Edward had at last written to her. She begged him to visit: 'Pray come, dear Edward, on Sunday, about three o'clock, and you can stop till five, for you can come any Sunday at these hours.' Someone, perhaps Peter Alley, had given her hopes of a reprieve—the prospect of a six-month prison sentence: 'Perhaps it is all for the best, for I am confident that it will make me both steady and penitent the rest of my life; though it's hard to suffer innocent,' she wrote.

He did not visit. Ten days later, Eliza had sunk into despondency: 'I have no hopes whatever… I am making my peace with God and hope to be in a better world, as I shall leave this world innocent of a crime that's alleged against me.' Edward again promised to visit and Eliza sent him detailed instructions on how to gain admittance to Newgate. If he visited at all, it was only once or twice. By 4 May she knew they were finished: 'I should never like a man that would forget me,' she wrote. He responded, excusing his failure: he had no time, he had enemies, he had sent a friend in his place, he had visited her father. Angry, she wrote him a final letter: 'I feel very much hurt at your being out, and could not spare one single hour with me.' She was glad he was friendly with her parents, 'for you can spend many hours with them, when I am no more'. She expected never to see him again, as 'the Report' was due any day and 'now I wait with impatience to know my fate'. The Report was the list of those convicted felons the Privy Council had chosen for execution or reprieve.

After Eliza's conviction there was a wave of interest in her case. The Recorder's conduct of the trial and the unfairness of the verdict attracted the attention not only of the newspapers but also of influential men. A letter to *The Morning Chronicle* pointed out that one member of the jury was deaf. There were doubts about the 'scientific' evidence given by Marshall. In response, rumours, misinformation and libels about Eliza swilled around the media, probably pushed by the Turners and Silvester. *The Observer* and *The Morning Post*, both in the pay of the government, published outright lies about her: she had been expelled from school for lying and 'lewdness', they said; her parents were—oh, the horrors—Irish Catholics.

In Newgate, Eliza's state of mind veered between despair and hope. She even wrote to Orlibar Turner asking him to sign a petition on her behalf. This would have saved her: the prosecutor's plea for mercy for the guilty, especially for an otherwise respectable young woman with no previous criminal history and convicted on circumstantial evidence alone, would have been irresistible.

Among those who were perturbed by the trial was an anonymous chemical expert who examined Marshall's claims that arsenic made dumplings fail to rise and turned knives black. He asked his own cook to make dumplings and was able to contaminate them with arsenic without her noticing. They rose perfectly and did not change the colour of the knives. He sent his findings to Lord Sidmouth, the Home Secretary, and, bringing his experimental dumplings with him, called on Orlibar Turner, hoping to persuade him to sign the petition to save Eliza. While they were in conversation, first Robert Turner and then Marshall arrived at the house, the latter then making a speedy departure. Just as the Turners were won over, declaring that they was ready to sign the petition, John Silvester, the Recorder himself, was announced.

The chemist now attempted to show Silvester his experiments and to explain that arsenic did not tarnish knives. Silvester would not have it and declared that he was leaving. Robert Turner showed him to the door and on his return said to his father: 'The Recorder says you must not sign any petition—if you do, it will throw suspicion on the rest of the family!' It was the death blow to Eliza's hopes. Orlibar must have realised that one of the people most at risk of accusation was his own son.

Among the men of standing who appealed for mercy for Eliza was the former barrister Basil Montagu, a co-founder of The Society for the Diffusion of Knowledge Upon the Punishment of Death and the Improvement of Prison Discipline (he wanted to end hanging for all offences except wilful and premeditated murder). He had uncovered evidence that Robert Turner had had a previous episode of mental instability, appearing 'wild' and 'deranged', threatening to kill his wife and himself. He sent his evidence to Silvester, who dismissed it as 'wholly useless'.

In France, on 15 June, Napoleon was defeated at the battle of Waterloo. A week later he abdicated. Britain was saved. Eliza, meanwhile, waited in her cell, now shared with Mary Ann Clarke, who had been sentenced to death for 'stealing in a dwelling house'. Here Eliza was visited by her parents and by a Chelsea doctor, Thomas Wansborough, who provided spiritual comfort.

On 19 July Eliza, along with Mary Ann and the other condemned felons, was called to a ward in Newgate where they were made to kneel on the floor. The Report had arrived. As was his duty, the Reverend Horace Cotton, the zealous Ordinary (Chaplain) of the Old Bailey, who was another personal friend of the Turners, went from one condemned prisoner to the next announcing to each their fate.

FIG.5 The Condemned Service at Newgate. Prisoners under sentence of death were obliged to sit around a symbolic coffin, and were haranged by the prison chaplain for their crimes. *From T. Rowlandson and A.A. Pugin (1809), The Microcosm of London. London: R. Ackerman. Author's collection*

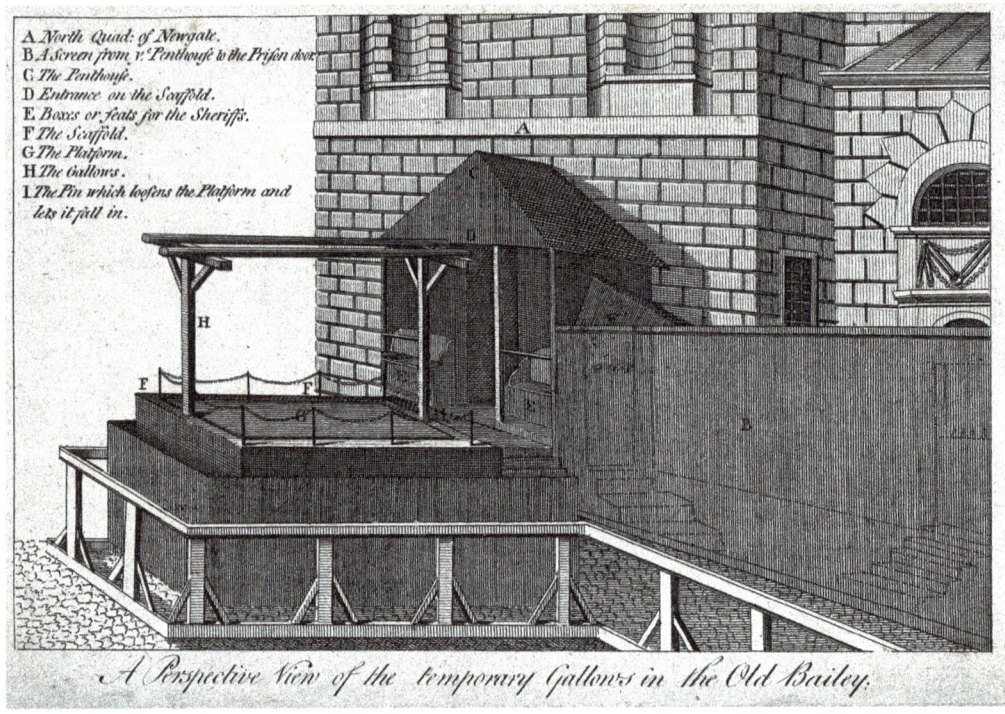

FIG.6 Death outside Newgate: Eliza Fenning, the two men also scheduled to die and the entourage of church ministers and officials emerged from Debtor's Door (behind the fence to the right), ascended the stairs and appeared on the platform in front of a huge crowd. *Wellcome Collection*

Mary Ann was reprieved. Not so, Eliza. 'Dearest and affectionate parents,' she wrote later, 'Let me entreat your immediate attendance to your lost child. Innocent, dear parents, I am, to God and man. Pray come soon. The report is come for me to be executed on Wednesday next.' Two days later, in a longer letter, she expressed her resignation and told them they would meet in heaven, where she would be united with her dead brothers and sisters. She wished them fortitude to bear the coming trauma.

In the meantime, she had to contend with the attentions of the Reverend Cotton. 'I am surely convinced that Mr Cotton is a great enemy to me,' she wrote on 29 June. His only purpose now was to persuade Eliza to admit her guilt and go to the gallows demonstrably penitent. The government did not want a repeat of the scenes at the execution outside Newgate in 1807 of convicted murderers John Holloway and Owen Haggerty. Ascending the platform in front of 40,000 people, Holloway shouted, 'Innocent! Innocent, Gentlemen! No verdict! Innocent, by God!', which he most probably was. The crowd surged and thirty-one people were killed and over forty injured.

Eliza would not go without the last word, however, and would not let her persecutors off the hook. 'I am murdered!' she wrote on 22 July, knowing that her letter would be published by her supporters after her death. She wanted to see the Turners in person, to ensure they were fully aware of the harm they had done her and sent a friend, possibly Mr Wansborough, to ask them to come to Newgate. Robert and Charlotte Turner arrived expecting contrition and a confession but were quickly disabused. Eliza was angry.

In her words: 'When Mr Turner came to me, he said, in the presence of Mr. Wansbury [Wansborough], he would do everything in his power to spare my life, but when going I refused my hand. I firmly and most solemnly declare to God and man, I am innocent of the crime, and how was it possible I could do it to a person who swore my life away, but may the Almighty God forgive them; believe me they are almost the death of my dear parents.'

She was avoiding Cotton, not only because she knew him to be allied with the Turners but also because he constantly urged her to confess. On the Sunday before her death, she was required to attend the condemned sermon in Newgate chapel, where she was to take the sacrament (*Fig.5*). This was always an event popular with the public, and the imminent hanging of a woman made it even more so. A huge number of people queued outside the gates for tickets and the chapel filled quickly. Twenty-one condemned prisoners entered and sat in the black pew set aside for them. Then those who were 'left for execution', Eliza and two others, William Oldfield, a child rapist, and Abraham Adams, convicted of sodomy, were brought in and the service began. When Cotton asked for prayers for 'those about to suffer' she could contain herself no longer and broke down into loud sobs. Cotton had chosen a text from Romans 6: 'What fruit had ye then in those things whereof ye are now ashamed? For the end of those things is death.' He alluded directly to her, saying that she had been persuaded by Satan that revenge was sweet and that he would protect her, but had then abandoned her. Eliza collapsed again. When the sacrament was given, the prisoners went to the altar, with Fenning protesting her innocence.

On Monday evening, Corbyn Lloyd, a Quaker banker, called on John Silvester, asking for a short respite to allow further investigations as there was no proof that it was Eliza, and no one else, who had poisoned the dumplings. Lloyd related the Recorder's response:

> Myself and my friend had done a great deal of harm by interesting ourselves about the girl, as it caused her to persist in denying her guilt; and the reason we felt so much interest about her was only because she was a pretty woman; and he felt so perfectly satisfied of her guilt (there never being a clearer case) that he knew no possible reason for delaying the execution.

On Tuesday, the day before her death, Eliza sent for Thomas King, the nervous apprentice. John Marshall, the surgeon who had attended the family when they fell ill, gave a second-hand account of this meeting, in which he described Eliza accusing King of the poisoning and King taking an oath in front of Mr Cotton to deny it. Later, Eliza took final leave of her parents. Her father asked her to be strong in the ordeal she was facing; her mother was distraught. In the condemned cell she wrote to her cellmate Mary Ann Clarke asking her not to grieve as her time 'is but short in this troublesome world, and I will soon be in eternal rest'. After her parents left, all that was left for Eliza to do was to pray, read her Bible and sleep.

ELIZA ROSE AT four to wash. She gave a lock of hair to each of the women prisoners who attended her. Her chosen minister could not be with her, so she was assigned Mr Vazie, whom she did not know. At six Mr Wansborough arrived to read the Bible with her. She was feeling faint and said it was all like a dream. It was now time to dress. She had chosen to die in a white muslin embroidered gown, tied with a white sash, and a matching cap. She put on lilac boots, laced in front. Shortly after eight, an officer tapped at the door and announced that it was time. Before she left on her final journey, she shouted 'Goodbye! Goodbye to all of you!' to the other prisoners.

She walked to the press room, the space where felons were prepared for the gallows. Oldfield and Adams were already there. 'Oh, Oldfield, you are going to heaven,' she said before John Langley, the hangman, started to pinion her arms, binding them by the elbows to her body. As Langley worked, Wansborough, probably by prior arrangement, asked if she was guilty. She announced loudly that 'Before God, I die innocent!' Eventually, a slow-moving and solemn cavalcade set off from the press room: the sheriffs and their officers, Wansborough, Vazie, and others, the Reverend Cotton enunciating the words of the burial service ('I am the resurrection and the life, saith the Lord'). When they came to Debtors Door (*Fig.6*), which opened on to the street, Wansborough took his leave. Before doing so, he again asked her about the crime, and once more she said, 'I die innocent.'

It was time. She went through the door. In front of her, filling every corner of the concourse, were thousands of spectators waiting in silence to witness the first execution of a woman at Newgate for three years. Eliza was nubile, attractive and religious. She had the bearing of a martyr. And quite apart from doubts about Eliza's guilt and sympathy for her fate, there would always be prurient interest in the mutilation of the body of a woman.

William Hone, the Radical, was there. 'I got into an immense crowd that carried me along with them against my will,' he wrote years later. 'At length I found myself under the gallows where Eliza Fenning was to be hanged. I had the greatest horror of witnessing an execution, and of this particular execution, a young girl of whose guilt I had grave doubts. But I could not help myself; I was closely wedged in; she was brought out. I saw nothing but I heard all.'

Thirty-five-year-old Hone was born in Bath although his family soon moved to London. His father, also called William, was a strictly religious Dissenter. At the age of twelve, already politicised and with a keen interest in the revolution in France, the younger Hone published a broadside on the freedoms of the English constitution. Soon afterwards, he began work as a legal copyist, his father's trade, but gradually he lost his religious faith and became involved with the controversial and radical London Corresponding Society, whose aims, which included universal male suffrage, alarmed the government. After an interlude in Chatham, where he was sent by his father in the hope that he would shake off his increasing radicalism, William returned to London and began several ventures, including opening a bookshop, a partnership with John Bone of the LCS. The business failed, like many of his other commercial projects, and Hone once more diversified, this time into the development of humanely-run asylums for the insane. He also became a campaigning journalist, holding the Establishment to account in the murder of Edward Vyse, the midshipman shot outside the house of the MP Frederick John Robinson, and, notably, the case of Eliza Fenning.[6]

Eliza was directed to ascend the scaffold first. She walked with purpose and took her place at the furthest end, standing erect and still. Cotton stood in front of her while Langley the hangman was behind her. He had come improperly prepared. He took a white cotton hood from his pocket and tried to put it over her head.[7] It was too small. He tried two others. They were also too small. Then he tied a muslin handkerchief over her face, but thought this would be inadequate and decided to put his own, dirty, pocket handkerchief across her eyes. Eliza's distress was palpable. 'Pray do not put it on,' she pleaded. 'Pray do not.' Cotton insisted: 'My dear, it must be on — he must put it on.' It was tied on. Langley then put the cord around her neck, threw the other end over the beam and secured it.

Oldfield now climbed the scaffold. He had requested to die next to Eliza and spoke to encourage her. Cotton moved off to attend to him and then to Abraham Adams, while Vazie stayed with Eliza, speaking into her ear. He was attempting to get her, even at this last opportunity, to confess. Cotton also tried again but her last words, before the platform fell, were 'I am innocent!' She was said not to have 'struggled' for long.

The three bodies were left to hang for the usual hour before being cut down. The corpses of murderers were sent to the College of Surgeons for dissection but none of the three dead felons had killed. Eliza's clothes were now the property of Langley the hangman, but her parents were at liberty to reclaim her body, provided they paid fourteen shillings and sixpence for 'Executioner's fees, stripping the body and the use of a shell [shroud]'. They were now utterly destitute, having sold everything they owned—watch, furniture, best clothes and, in William Fenning's phrase, 'the last shift from off the back of her mother'. They had even pawned their blankets and bedding and were forced to sleep on the floor, but they managed to borrow the fee and Eliza's body was laid out in the back room of their lodgings.

Small crowds of wellwishers assembled outside their home. Some were admitted and allowed to view the body but then police officers arrived. 'The magistrates have ordered that nobody shall go into the house,' they told William Hone when he came to pay his respects. He told the officers that the order was illegal and ignored it.

Eliza's funeral followed four days later. A hundred mourners accompanied her bier, which was carried to the church of St George the Martyr near Brunswick Square by six young women dressed in white. A substantial crowd gathered at the burial ground but again police officers tried to obstruct the way, insisting they could not go in. Although the ceremony passed off without major incident, the anger of the populace was intense and growing and a thousand people gathered outside the Turners' house in Chancery Lane. There were threats to burn it down. Some people were arrested for behaving in a 'riotous and tumultuous manner' and the police were on guard there for days.

Eliza's case continued to trouble and intrigue lawyers and scientists for months, even years, afterwards. Scores of pamphlets were published. William Hone started gathering evidence that would make it clear who was responsible for the unnecessary destruction of a young woman in the prime of life. His *Important Results of an Elaborate Investigation into the Mysterious Case of Elizabeth Fenning*,[8] published by John Watkins, was a detailed investigation into the collusion between the Turners and Silvester. Charlotte Turner and her servant Sarah Peer had lied about the delivery of coal to the household that morning, their movements in and out of the kitchen and the appearance of the dumplings; essential witnesses (Thomas King, the apprentice, and Henry Ogilvy, the apothecary who had first treated those poisoned) had deliberately not been called; John Marshall was allowed to give scientific (but totally wrong) evidence; Silvester's extraordinary intervention in the incident with Orlibar Turner and the petition and Basil Montagu's probing into Robert Turner's mental ill-health were set out in detail.

As Radicals and reformers wrote pamphlets and editorials about Eliza, Silvester, Marshall and the Turner family sought to limit the damage to their reputations. *The Observer* continued to publish more lies about the Fennings. They were said to have put Eliza's body on display in return for money. A turnkey at Newgate was persuaded to sign an affidavit to say that Eliza's father had urged her to protest her innocence, not because he believed her to be blameless but in order to preserve his own reputation. William Fenning was forced to issue an affidavit of his own in answer. John Marshall's pamphlet *Five Cases of Recovery from the Effects of Arsenic*[9] described his treatment of the Turners and Eliza Fenning on the night of the poisoning and his experiments on the remains of the dumplings and asserted that Eliza was clearly guilty. It was greeted with incredulity by Eliza's supporters. Marshall claimed that Eliza had wanted to kill herself after she poisoned the family in order to evade justice and had eaten her dumpling only after Roger Gadsden had eaten his (untrue—she had eaten it before) and that her lack of 'humanity' was shown in her refusal to help the pregnant Charlotte Turner after she fell ill. *The Independent Whig* took him to task, calling his assertions 'spurious' and 'flimsy', and it pointed to another disturbing case of a female servant accused of poisoning her employer's family who was currently in prison and awaiting trial.

SEVEN WEEKS AFTER Eliza Fenning was hanged, Anne Newman, accompanied by her maid Mary Eades, took her two young daughters for an evening walk near her home in Kennington, Surrey, on the south side of the Thames. Anne was married to Richard Newman, a butcher, who had had a problem with rats, which plagued his house and the adjacent slaughterhouse. His rat-catcher put arsenic behind the skirting boards, under the flagstones and in the suet drawer in the kitchen. When Mary Eades came across a twist of paper on a window-sill, one of Mr Newman's slaughtermen told her it was poison and not to touch it.

After their walk, Anne Newman asked her second servant, nineteen-year-old Elizabeth Miller, to bring some watery gruel (a thin porridge) upstairs for the children's supper, which she did. Mary Eades added magnesia and rhubarb to it. Although the toddler, Elizabeth Ann, was quite well, Mary, the baby, had been sickening and the hope was that this would settle her. Both little girls drank the gruel and Mary Eades had some of it too. As she dressed the baby for bed, she felt sick, with a burning sensation in her throat and stomach. Very soon, highly distressed, little Elizabeth Ann ran in to her mother. She climbed into her lap for comfort and started vomiting, as did the baby.

Soon afterwards, Richard Newman, the children's father, came up.

'What have you been doing with the gruel?' he demanded of Elizabeth Miller.

'Nothing,' said Elizabeth and continued to vehemently deny doing anything wrong. Eventually she burst into tears.

The basin of gruel was brought from the kitchen and Newman challenged her to drink it, but by then she had seen that the children and Mary Eades were ill and refused. Newman sent her for the apothecary, a Mr Dixon. During their journey back to Kennington, Elizabeth told him that she had made the gruel and thickened it with oatmeal she had found in a jar in the kitchen cupboard. One of the men employed by Newman had brought it in about a month before to treat a cold, she said. Dixon ordered the basin of gruel and all the equipment and utensils involved to be locked up for future examination. Later he analysed the contents of the basin in the presence of 'four philosophical gentlemen [natural scientists],' who found that it was 'strongly impregnated with arsenic'—but, like Marshall's, this was worthless science.

As both children continued to deteriorate, Elizabeth was sent out to fetch medicine. At nine o'clock the following morning, after fitting several times, Elizabeth Ann died.

An inquest was held at the White Hart pub, a few doors away from the Newmans' home, in front of Charles Jemmett, the Surrey coroner. Anne Newman told the jury that Elizabeth Miller was a bad-tempered girl who was often cross with the children, and that Elizabeth Ann had not liked her. The previous Monday, she said, she had scolded her twice for 'suffering the men in the shop to take improper liberties with her'. These were echoes of the accusation against Eliza. Did a humiliating telling-off provoke a murderous resentment of her mistress?[10] The case came to trial the following April at Kingston, Surrey, heard by Charles Abbott. William Hone was among the observers. Elizabeth was defended by Mr Nolan, whose bill was being paid for by a public subscription; a solicitor gave his services for free. Isaac Espinasse, representing

Richard Newman, described the abuse the butcher had suffered for his prosecution of Elizabeth. He had been 'assailed on all hands' and had been 'foully traduced, and vitally injured in his trade'. Elizabeth was acquitted and Justice Abbott stated that the child had died as the result of an accident. Elizabeth had simply mistaken arsenic for oatmeal.

Had justice been done? It is impossible to know but no one had seen Elizabeth add arsenic to the gruel. Perhaps mindful of the catastrophic verdict against Eliza, the jurymen were cautious.

For Hone, the acquittal of Elizabeth Miller was an opportunity to remind the public of the behaviour of Orlibar Turner and his family towards Eliza. He published his account of Elizabeth Miller's trial in several forms, including the pamphlet *Four Important Trials at Kingston Assizes, April 5th 1816*[11] in which he detailed thirteen examples of Mr Turner's deliberate concealment of pertinent facts during the Fenning case, among them the refusal to allow Eliza's father to see her when she herself was suffering the effects of arsenic poisoning; his decision to employ as his solicitor the magistrate's clerk who had taken Eliza's deposition; and his failure to inform the court of a possible suspect within his own family, his son Robert. At this distance of time, we cannot be sure that arsenic killed Elizabeth Ann Newman just as we cannot be sure it was in the dumplings Eliza made. As Marshall's experiments showed, the science of detecting poisons was rudimentary; Eliza's prosecution provided a salutary lesson in its limitations. It was at least twenty years before an effective test for arsenic became available.

Eliza Fenning's memory lived on for decades, in stage plays and books. Struck by the similarities between her story and the plot of *La Pie Voleuse*, a melodrama then playing to enthusiastic audiences in London, Hone wrote a prose version, *The Narrative of the Magpie, or the Maid of Palaiseau*.[12] Eliza inspired other characters too: Mary Shelley may have used her as a model for Justine Moritz, a servant girl in her gothic novel *Frankenstein*, who is unjustly accused of a murder the monster has committed, is pressurised into confessing and hangs, condemned by a cold-hearted judge. Plays about *Eliza Fenning, the Persecuted Servant Girl* were being performed well into the 1850s and in 1867 Charles Dickens commissioned seasoned journalist Water Thornbury to write about the case for his magazine *All the Year Round*. Thornbury concluded that Eliza was an 'entirely guiltless young creature'.[13]

By contrast, the reputations and fortunes of her accusers suffered.

In 1825 Orlibar Turner was declared bankrupt. In 1828, John Gordon Smith, the University of London's first Professor of Medical Jurisprudence, noted a claim in *The Morning Journal* that Robert Turner had died in Ipswich workhouse confessing that he had put arsenic in the dumplings. Robert was certainly living in the area in 1820 (his wife Charlotte was originally from Suffolk), but we know no more than that.

In 1829 *The Examiner* reported that William Fenning, Eliza's heartbroken father, was still living in London. 'The unfortunate girl was his favourite child,' the paper said, forgetting that in 1815 she was also his only surviving offspring. A man called William Fenning died in Holborn in London in 1842. If this is 'our' William Fenning, he would have been ninety-one.

We will never know what actually happened in the kitchen of 68 Chancery Lane that day in March 1815 when the coal man called and Eliza was making dumplings. Perhaps Thomas King, the apprentice so shy he could barely speak, thought it would be fun to observe the effects of a few grains of arsenic on the stomachs of his master's family and underestimated their power. Perhaps Robert Turner, in one of his periods of instability, slipped into the kitchen while Eliza went to fetch the steaks and wrought the damage. It doesn't really matter who did it. It is enough to know that Eliza probably did not.

Eliza had the misfortune to be accused at a time when the middle class were on high alert. On the day the dumplings were poisoned, Bonaparte was reported to be on his way to Paris and Wellington was making for Belgium to coordinate the Allies' response. The earlier certainties, of a safe, free and stable Britain, looked suddenly in doubt. The middle class was gripped by a loss of confidence, seeing danger everywhere, in the Corn Law rioters' ripping up of iron railings and turning them into spears, in the Radicals and their clamour for reform and change, and in an impudent servant in Chancery Lane who could read the writing on a packet of poison.

LOVE & LIES
in the age of ELOPEMENT

IN THE EARLY hours of 22 September 1817, in a townhouse in Taunton, Somerset, Jane Marke, a domestic servant, crept into the darkness of the first-floor bedroom in which her master's two young daughters and sixteen-year-old niece were sleeping. Careful not to wake the young ones, Jane urgently shook the teenager awake, pulled a frock over her head and, whispering dire threats if she cried out, bustled her through a downstairs window to a group of people waiting outside. Two days later the teenager, whose name was Maria Glenn, was traced to a house thirty miles away, and brought back to her family in a dishevelled and traumatised state.

Maria told her uncle, George Lowman Tuckett, a barrister on the Western Circuit, that her kidnappers were the Bowditches, the family of yeoman farmers with whom she had lodged during the summer while recuperating from whooping cough, and that they had tried, unsuccessfully, to force her to marry twenty-five-year-old James Bowditch—because they believed her to be an heiress. At the time, a woman's wealth, unless protected by trusts, automatically became the property of the man she married.

There the story might have ended, with Mr Tuckett salvaging what remained of Maria's reputation by sending her away to relatives or even consenting to a hasty marriage with James Bowditch. After all,

FIG.1 Tales of naïve young boarding-school girls absconding with eager but impoverished chancers gave scope for plenty of prurient speculation. *The Elopement by Thomas Rowlandson (1792). Watercolour with pen and gray and black ink. Yale Center for British Art, Paul Mellon Collection. B1977.14.346*

she had spent two nights away from home, unchaperoned. Tuckett opted instead to prosecute Maria's abductors for kidnap, assault and conspiracy. It was an unusual decision. Most families tried to keep a lid on news about absconding or stolen daughters (and occasionally sons) but Tuckett's determination to pursue Maria's tormentors through the courts meant that every aspect of his niece's character and behaviour could be reported on and discussed in sitting rooms, pubs and clubs across the country.

On a stiflingly hot August day in 1818, the ten defendants who were alleged to have been involved in the conspiracy to abduct Maria appeared at Dorchester assizes, where the trial was heard at the Court of King's Bench. The event promised, and delivered, high drama laced with an intoxicating mix of class, money and sex. For Maria, who was so shy that she usually hid her face within the brim of a poke bonnet, the experience of sitting in the witness box in a packed and hot court speaking about what had happened to her almost a year previously must have been agony. The story she related was astonishing: before her disappearance, she claimed, members of the Bowditch family and their friends had followed her around Taunton, harassed her into signing fake legal documents and threatened her with death if she told her uncle about the plan to carry her off and marry her to James; during her kidnap they had drugged, berated and bullied her and made her to stand in front of a man pretending to be a minister of the church who conducted a sham marriage.

The Bowditches' defence was that this had not been an abduction at all but an elopement, and all of it had been Maria's own idea. They aimed to shred Maria's reputation by implying that she should have been grateful for the interest James, a 'well-looking' young man, took in her (even her uncle judged Maria to be 'plain'). The Bowditches' witnesses, most of them relatives or employees, accused her of improper behaviour with James, of flirting with him and meeting him in secret without her bonnet and shawl.[14]

THE PUBLIC WAS well versed in the elopement trope—the secret romance, the plan, the anxious wait by the window, the tread on the gravel, the knotted sheets, the readied chaise, the complicit friend or servant, and finally the dash for the Scottish border to stand in front of the famed blacksmith and his anvil. It was embedded in popular culture, a frequent theme on stage, in books and even on the walls of countless homes. Paintings of 'runaway marriages' were hung in genteel homes and cheap prints showing fleeing couples tearing through the countryside in chaises were found in the parlours of modest houses and cottages. The subject also featured in the plots of a slew of comedies, musical farces and operettas. Richard Brinsley Sheridan explored the comic potential of elopement in *The Rivals* and revisited it in his libretto for the hugely popular comic opera *The Duenna, or the Double Elopement*. Elopement was even the theme for a board game, 'The New game of elopement or A trip to Gretna Green. Designed & invented to enliven the winter evenings,' published in 1820, in which players moved through stages labelled The Alarm, The Pursuit, The Flight until, after reaching Carlisle Bridge and fighting off the Interception, they are Married.[15]

Wide disparity in the class of the parties involved added extra piquancy. The young Jane Austen dropped into her story *Frederic and Elfrida* the fact that the eldest Miss Fitzroy had run off with the coachman. She also alluded to elopement in her story *Jack and Alice: A Novel* when Lady Williams describes the last words of her governess:

> 'Under her tuition I daily became more amiable, and might perhaps
> by this time have nearly attained perfection, had not my worthy
> Preceptoress been torn from my arms e'er I had attained my
> seventeenth year. I never shall forget her last words. "My dear Kitty"
> she said "Good night t'ye." I never saw her afterwards,' continued Lady
> Williams, wiping her eyes, 'She eloped with the Butler the same night.'[16]

Of course, it was not so funny if your own daughter or ward eloped. In 1791 newly-minted heiress Clementina Clarke, a tender fourteen, was inveigled into getting into a chaise parked outside her Bristol boarding school by local apothecary Richard Vining Perry and whisked off to be forcibly married at Gretna Green. Just like Maria Glenn, she was powerless to stop others from taking action against her abductor. Her schoolmistress, Selina Mills, who had tried in vain to retrieve Clementina from Perry's clutches, took it upon herself two years later to prosecute him at Bristol Assizes for feloniously stealing her pupil and marrying her against her consent, a capital charge. The strategy backfired. Clementina, now aged seventeen and pregnant with her second child, did the only thing she could. She refused to cooperate with the prosecution. If Perry had been found guilty, the marriage would have been annulled and her children bastardised; there was also a risk that her husband would be executed—further ignominy. Unsurprisingly, Perry was acquitted. Sadly, life did not improve for Clementina after the trial. As her husband, Perry was entitled to everything she owned and he soon abandoned her to poverty and an early death.[17]

In her later work, Jane Austen explored some of the negative consequences of fugitive marriage—in *Mansfield Park* Frances Price's mother's reward for marrying in haste without the consent of her family is ten children and a life of poverty with her disabled, alcoholic husband —and she understood that women were vulnerable both for their fortunes and lack of them. In *Pride and Prejudice* the best outcome for penniless Lydia Bennet after her flight with George Wickham is to marry the man who has ruined her reputation, only possible because Darcy has made a marriage settlement on her. Austen's heroes also show remarkable forbearance when beloved women succumb to grooming and deception by unscrupulous fortune-seekers. Darcy stands by his sister Georgiana after her entanglement with Wickham and in *Sense and Sensibility* Colonel Brandon supports the daughter of his former love Eliza and marries Marianne, both of them Willoughby's victims.

ELOPEMENTS AND THEIR darker flipside, abductions, have occurred throughout history, but in the mid and late Georgian era there was a pronounced increase in their frequency. It is impossible to calculate exact numbers but between 1794 and 1895 about ten thousand marriages are listed in a log kept by David and Simon Lang, so-called blacksmith parsons at Gretna Green.[18] It is estimated that the collection represents only half the number of marriages conducted this way, which would give, as a rough calculation, at least two hundred marriages a year. The true figure would have been considerably higher: Gretna was by no means the only Scottish border village receiving runaway couples.

What was behind this explosion in fugitive marriage? Ironically, it arose from an attempt to regularise the marriage laws. Lord Hardwicke's 1753 Act sought to end clandestine unions such as those taking place within the 'rules' of the Fleet in London, an area where the normal rules of matrimony did not apply and where even defrocked priests could marry couples, and to impose order on the ramshackle system operated by parishes. Now couples were obliged to register four weeks in advance or sign a bond to swear that at least one party had lived in the parish for at least four weeks. Under-twenty-ones had to have the consent of parents or guardians. But this law did not apply in Scotland, where the age of consent was twelve for girls and fourteen for boys, nor at destinations overseas.

The 1753 Act was not greeted enthusiastically by all. On its passage through the Commons it was criticised not because it thwarted young love but because it seemed to be a plot to 'secure all the rich heiresses in the kingdom for the aristocracy'. Clandestine marriage was an acceptable form of social advancement and, critics argued, men should be cheered on in their pursuit of higher-class women, not prosecuted or incarcerated for it. After his acquittal at Bristol, Richard Vining Perry was carried through the streets by a jubilant mob. He was, after all, merely looking out for himself. Clementina was a prize and any man would snare a similar one if he could.

Maria's uncle George Tuckett surely knew about Clementina's ordeal and Perry's triumph. The case was widely reported in the papers, and salacious satirical prints depicting Selina Mills, Clementina and Perry were on sale in print shops. Tuckett may actually have been in the courtroom at Bristol in 1794 when Perry was tried. He took his pupillage with Sir Vicary Gibbs, the judge. So, knowing the reputational risk to Maria, why did he persist in his prosecution? He was certainly motivated by a desire for retribution, fuelled by a fervent, almost religious, belief in truth and the rule of law. From the beginning he was solidly supportive of Maria and believed her story, but he misjudged the cynicism with which it would be received.

Georgian society liked females to be compliant, virtuous and chaste while simultaneously regarding them as the natural inheritors of Eve—devious, duplicitous and lustful. Although Maria appeared to have been vindicated when four of the ten defendants at the Dorchester trial were sentenced to prison terms, doubts about her testimony, fanned by the Bowditch family and their friends, soon spread. The memory of two notorious cases of teenage girls reinforced the public's assumption that females, particularly young ones, were natural liars. On New Year's Day 1753, seventeen-year-old scullery maid Elizabeth Canning (*Fig.2*) went missing in east London. When she returned a month later, she told an

FIGS. 2 & 3 Elizabeth Canning (*above*) and Princess Caraboo, notorious teen liars whose reputations cast a shadow over Maria Glenn's account of her ordeal. *From James Caulfield (1820), Portraits, Memoirs and Characters from the Revolution of 1688 to the End of the Reign of George II, Vol 3. London: T.H. Whitely; Sabine Baring-Gould (1908), 'Devonshire Characters and Strange Events'. London: J. Lane*

ever-shifting and frankly unbelievable story of kidnap and imprisonment in a hayloft and a diet of bread and water. There followed a series of events that could have been avoided with a simple 'sense check'. Two elderly women, identified more or less at random, were capitally tried for stealing Canning's stays: one was imprisoned, the other branded. Three men from Dorset, witnesses for the defence who had travelled up to London to swear that the accused women were elsewhere at the time of the alleged kidnapping, were charged with perjury. Eventually, after a blizzard of pamphlets both supporting and opposing Canning, common sense prevailed. The Dorset men were acquitted while Canning was tried for perjury and found guilty. She was transported to the American colonies.[19] The other notable lesson in girls' fibbing occurred only six months before Maria's disappearance, when the nation was transfixed by the story of 'Princess Caraboo' from 'Javasu' (*Fig.3*) who had turned up in the village of Almondsbury in Gloucestershire, only fifty miles from Taunton. After a Bristol lodging-house keeper recognised her description in the newspaper, this mysterious figure was unmasked as Mary Willcocks, a cobbler's daughter, who was soon afterwards quietly hustled off to America in the care of three strictly religious ladies.[20]

As it turned out, Maria also ended up in exile. Helped by powerful figures in Taunton, the Bowditches prosecuted her for perjury. She was found guilty but before she was due to be sentenced Tuckett whisked her off to France, where she lived in exile for many years.

THE BRUTAL TREATMENT of Maria Glenn by her alleged abductors was outdone nine years later in the so-called Shrigley abduction. Fifteen-year-old heiress and only child Ellen Turner of Pott Shrigley in Cheshire was taken from her Liverpool boarding school by Edward Gibbon Wakefield, a thirty-year-old widower. He had form. At the age of twenty, he had eloped with seventeen-year-old heiress Eliza Pattle, whose widowed mother afterwards accepted the marriage and settled £70,000 on her daughter. In 1820 Eliza died in childbirth leaving him with two small children. Wakefield, who had never previously met Ellen, stooped to astonishing levels of cruelty to deceive her. He sent his servant with a carriage to present a message to her schoolmistresses, stating that her mother had become paralysed and wished to see her daughter immediately. Then he told Ellen that her mother was well but her father's business had collapsed. The next day, he told her that her father would be rescued from his creditors only if she consented to marry him. Two banks had agreed that some of her father's estate would be transferred to her, or rather, to her husband. They married at Gretna Green, after which Wakefield fled with his bounty to France. The marriage was later annulled by Parliament and Ellen was legally married two years later, at the age of seventeen, to a wealthy neighbour. Wakefield and his brother William, who had helped him, were convicted at trial and sentenced to three years in Newgate.[21]

Wakefield's abduction of Ellen Turner and the subsequent trial was the last major case of its kind. Even the 'extraordinary' case in 1842 of Ann Crellin, a wealthy Liverpudlian spinster who prosecuted eight people for conspiring to take her away to Gretna Green and forcibly marry her to one of the gang, John Orr M'Gill, did not measure up. She was short, stout and forty and her suitor was a handsome thirty-year-old Irishman, so there was plenty of amusement for the public, especially when they read that Ann was seen with her head on M'Gill's knees and to order and consume six or seven brandies on the trot. The jury were unimpressed and when delivering their guilty verdict against four of the gang the foreman told the judge that 'Miss Crellin is also herself highly culpable in the business'. The sentences handed down were comparatively light: two of the men were given imprisonment of eighteen and fifteen months and the others hard labour for two and twelve months. The case served as a depressing example of the financial helplessness of women after marriage. Until their marriage was dissolved, M'Gill was still Ann's husband. When he was incarcerated in prison awaiting trial for forcibly marrying her, he was able to instruct her bankers not to pay out her own money to her. She had to sue him for it.[22]

IN FRANCE, THE exiled Maria Glenn married and bore three children. After she was widowed she married for a second time and produced a daughter, but the relationship with her husband failed and in around 1848 she slipped back into England, settling first near Kennington Common in south London and later in Canterbury, where she died of a heart attack in 1866. The story she passed down to her descendants was that she had been sent to France for her education – the stigma of what

FIG.4 Maria Glenn in the 1860s. After the breakdown of her second marriage she returned to England discreetly and never told her children the true reason for her exile in France. *Courtesy of the Hudson family*

FIG. 5 A False Alarm on the Road to Gretna 'tis only the Mail! (1838)
Print by Richard Gilson Reeve aft. Charles B. Newhouse. Yale Center for British Art, Paul Mellon Collection. B1985.36.744

had happened to her at Taunton, her subsequent vilification and flight were too shameful to confess.

The fashion for romantic elopements declined as the nineteenth century wore on, especially after 1856 when Scottish law was changed to require twenty-one days' residence before marriage. Eventually, the Georgian period, and especially the Regency, came to be viewed with nostalgia as the golden age of runaway marriages, when true love won out against unwarranted family opposition. Now, elopement is a term used by the wedding sector keen to sell an extra frisson to engaged couples planning their big day. It means, merely, marrying far from home, perhaps on a beach or at a luxury hotel, witnessed by a few guests. It was once a more potent term, with the potential to make a fortune or ruin a life.

SUSANNA MEREDITH
THE PRISONERS' FRIEND

NEXT TIME YOU find yourself in the upper end of Wandsworth Road near the grimy traffic interchange at Vauxhall, stop near the entrance of Nine Elms tube station and look across the road towards the railway bridge. Half-close your eyes and picture a shabby Victorian building set back from the road. You might also be able to imagine the shouts and raucous laughter of women working in the back of the house and, on the air, a mix of starch and bleach. You are looking at the site of the Nine Elms Laundry, which stood there for most of the last quarter of the nineteenth century, an extraordinary enterprise staffed by former prisoners and run by an extraordinary woman: Susanna Meredith.

Mrs Meredith was born Susanna Lloyd in Cork, Ireland in 1823, the eldest daughter of Farmar Lloyd, the governor of Cork County Gaol. At the age of seventeen she married William Lambert Meredith, a doctor ten years her senior with whom she shared a fervent Protestant faith. He died only seven years later. Childless, she threw herself into philanthropic work. In Cork, in an effort to mitigate the effects of the Great Famine, she became involved in an industrial school for three hundred girls who were taught lacemaking, and in London—she and her widowed mother moved there in 1860—she edited *The Alexandra*, a magazine advocating greater employment opportunities for women.[23]

FIG.1 In the latter part of the nineteenth century, Susanna Meredith was a pioneer in the aftercare of women prisoners. *From E.M. Tomkinson (1887), The World's Workers. London: Cassell & Company*

FIG.2 Women serving sentences of hard labour work in the laundry at Woking Convict Prison. *Drawing by Paul Renouard, published in 'The Graphic', 7 September 1889*

However, it was for her work with women former prisoners in south London that she was best known.

Dismayed at the misery she found when she started visiting women incarcerated in Brixton Prison (at that time for women only), she and a group of like-minded middle-class women established the Prison Mission.[24] Every morning two volunteers stood by the gates of London prisons that accommodated women to await those released that day. Some who emerged were persuaded to accompany the ladies to rooms nearby. Of course, they may have relished the thought of a Bible reading and prayer but it is more likely that they were primarily attracted by the offer of food and work.[25]

The work was sewing, at which few of the women excelled and which brought the Mission pitifully little revenue. Mrs Meredith and her fellow volunteers decided to change tack and developed more ambitious plans.

> [Mrs Meredith] has always maintained that the only way to wean a convict from evil ways and to help her to a respectable place in the world is to inculcate habits of industry.
>
> *Mother's Companion,* 1 February 1895

THE VICTORIANS WERE obsessed with crime and the 'criminal classes', and especially criminal women. An ideal understanding of womanhood prevailed; women were designed by God to be naturally maternal, gentle, caring, loving helpmeets for men. By breaking the law of the land they also broke the laws of nature; they became, in effect, 'unsexed' monsters. Although far fewer women broke the law than men (their crimes were overwhelmingly larceny or low-level violence, often connected with alcohol use) and fewer of them were imprisoned, those who did transgress were considered more morally depraved than men and, in general, deserving of harsher punishments.

When transportation to the colonies ended in 1857 the government was faced with the problem of how to deal with the thousands of additional prisoners on its hands.[26] The focus began to be on preventative measures, including ways to reduce the rate of recidivism. In almost every county there were Discharged Prisoners' Aid Societies, licensed by the Home Office, whose aim was to find work and accommodation for convicts who had been released early under the ticket-of-leave system.

While they were in the societies' care convicts were still under sentence and could be returned to prison if they broke the terms of their release. In London the Royal Society for the Assistance of Discharged Prisoners, founded in 1857, operated a hostel for women at Russell House in Streatham, south London, where it trained them as domestic servants and helped them to emigrate to Canada or the United States.[27]

Mrs Meredith knew that attempting to place female former prisoners as servants within households had a high risk of failure. Some of the women received weekly visits from the police and there was also the fundamental issue of trust. In 1879, she wrote:

> It would be well to make it generally known that only a very small percentage of women who have suffered penal servitude enter the domestic line of life. They are usually incapable of such employment. Their way of getting an honest living is mostly confined to daily labour in such operations as women with characters for propriety can afford to refuse. Happily there is no lack of work accessible to convicted women, without their competing for domestic service. When they attempt this, it is usually with the aid of misdirected benevolence, or by false statements. It is unwise and unnecessary to place them in families. Their labour should be encouraged in other directions, under circumstances that provide for their special disqualifications.
>
> *Evening Standard*, 2 August 1879

With six other women, including her unmarried older sister Martha, Mrs Meredith set up the Discharged Female Prisoners' Aid Society. The 'other directions' Mrs Meredith had in mind was the Society's own steam laundry, which would employ the women directly.

Laundries had played a role in punishment and rehabilitation since the eighteenth century, mainly housing so-called fallen women. The first Magdalene laundry, a Protestant institution, was established in Whitechapel in London in 1758. By the first half of the nineteenth century, Magdalene laundries operated as penitentiary workhouses. In Ireland Catholic Magdalene laundries proliferated and focused on recalcitrant teenagers and unwed mothers. Mrs Meredith's operation, established in the late 1860s at Nine Elms House, 6 Upper Belmont Terrace, Wandsworth Road, was run on very different lines.

Near to the Nine Elms Station,[28] and adjoining a bridge over the South Western Railway, is a brick house, standing in an enclosure, which has evidently seen better days [...] The interior of the house is rather dreary and uninviting. There is no trace of luxury in the appointments. On the left-hand of the entrance hall is an uncarpeted room, in which several wooden chairs are placed in rows, giving to it the look of a school-house in a poor neighbourhood. Here instruction, chiefly of an elementary religious kind, is imparted to adult women, by ladies who eschew preaching or lecturing [...] At the back of the house, in what had formerly been a good-sized garden, are long iron sheds, in which clothes are disinfected, washed, mangled and dried. In the space left vacant the wet clothes are dried when the weather is fine; when rain falls they are dried in artificially heated chambers.

The Daily News, 25 July 1871

The women were governed by a set of rules, prominently displayed. They had to do all the work assigned to them, were not allowed alcohol, could not carry money on their person, and were forbidden from leaving the premises without permission. Breaking the rules could lead to instant dismissal, but the regime was firm rather than strict. Women who served a subsequent prison term were free to come back to the laundry, an important point of difference to other discharged prisoners' associations, and women remanded by the courts were also accepted. There was no religious barrier. Everyone was welcomed, whatever their affiliation.

The women worked a ten-hour day from eight in the morning to six in the evening for which they received a shilling and sixpence (7.5p) a day; fourpence was deducted for accommodation.[29] Most of the women lodged with local families, with a handful living on the premises at Nine Elms House. As you might expect, some women had difficulty conforming. They failed to turn up, or relapsed into crime, drink or sex work, or stole from the laundry. For example, in 1881 Ellen Davis was sentenced to five years penal servitude for taking two towels and some linen, 'the property of Mrs Meredith'.[30] We do not know whether Mrs Meredith approved of the harshness of the sentence.

Initially, the laundry was set up to be self-financing and washed for the well-off in the neighbourhood, but when the prisoners complained that their middle-class customers expected them to be grateful for the opportunity to wash for them, Mrs Meredith decided that they would take in the washing of the needy and sick instead. Washing was often fraught with difficulty for poor households, who had few clothes or bedclothes and could not dry items fast enough to use them. Mrs Meredith offered families suffering infectious disease or cancer a free service. She came to call this 'washing for love'.[31]

The 1871 census shows Mrs Meredith and her sister Martha living within walking distance of the laundry at 45 The Lawns, South Lambeth Road, with four domestic servants.[32] By this time, she and Martha had started another ground-breaking initiative, a natural extension of their work with convict women. Troubled by the plight of the prisoners' children, the girls in particular, they developed plans for a permanent children's home outside London.[33] This was unprecedented. There was little official interest in the welfare of prisoners' children, except when they became criminals themselves. In 1870, with her friend Caroline Cavendish (1840–1925), Mrs Meredith started placing very young children with foster parents in the area around Chertsey, Surrey, and a year later, with donations and government support, set up Princess Mary Village Homes for Girls at nearby Addlestone. The Homes were run on the cottage or 'family' system, with each house-mother in charge of ten girls.[34] By 1880 the Homes were caring for around 175 girls.[35]

Many of the women whose children were being taken into care objected. 'It is with great difficulty that we can prevail on these women to give their little girls out of their hands,' one of Mrs Meredith's associates told *The Daily News* in 1871, blaming the women's 'cruel thirst for profit through their means' rather than the strength of their maternal attachment. 'The mothers are insensible to our sense of their guilt,' she went on. 'Some smile at us; many are quite annoyed at our suggestions. Some have violently resisted our attempts to rescue their own daughters from defilement.'[36]

In London the mission at Nine Elms House was expanding. After a fund-raising drive, the washing sheds were rebuilt in 1872. In 1878 a coffee hall and a reading room were added; they proved popular with local railway workers and their families.[37] A Wesleyan commissioner who visited in 1883 had mixed feelings about the operation, however. In a piece titled 'Among the Sick and the Sinful' he described Mrs

Meredith's work as 'one of the most beautiful and blessed manifestations of the power of the love of Christ'; but he found the plain brick building, reached via 'dingy' Wandsworth Road, 'dreadfully dull' and in need of brightening up. As he observed a volunteer read a story to about thirty women while they had their lunch—Mrs Meredith, ever the pragmatist, felt that too much religion could defeat her aim of converting them—he came to the conclusion that 'for the most part [the women] obviously belonged to the lower, if not the lowest class' and that 'only one or two bore any traces of refinement'.[38]

The women's appearance was of central importance to respectable society. Most people believed that if you looked evil you were evil and that attractive criminals were merely expert in hiding their criminal souls. In the late nineteenth century two allied theories of biological determinism became increasingly influential. Physiognomy, the study of the correspondence between facial features or body structure and psychological characteristics, exposed women, especially criminal women, to lengthy discussions and analysis of their appearance and moral value. Female offenders, most of whom had lived chaotic lives marked by poverty, violence and disadvantage, were judged against the unattainable standards of beauty of the middle and upper classes.

Alongside physiognomy sat eugenics, the racist and classist theory that society would be improved by the elimination of those with weak or criminal genes, which was boosted in Britain by, among others, the sexologist and social reformer Havelock Ellis. He believed that physical markers indicated specific criminality: infanticides had more down on their faces and female thieves went grey more quickly, were uglier and exhibited signs of degeneracy in their sexual organs earlier than other women. He had cause for hope, however—he thought female criminals so disgusting that men would not procreate with them and the criminal classes would eventually disappear.[39]

Everything about the physical state of criminal women was scrutinised for clues to their inner character. Journalists visiting the laundry felt that their readers were owed descriptions of the women's appearance. 'All have an animal look in their eyes,' wrote *The Daily News*'s correspondent in 1871. 'A heaviness of feature is common to them all... If the faces of these women were dyed a copper-colour, and if they were dressed in nondescript garments of a female Ute, or Shoshone

Indian, they would pass for genuine savages. In reality they are not much better.'[40] In her 1881 *A Book About Criminals*,[41] Mrs Meredith acknowledged that the bodies of criminals were public property.

> His [the criminal's] likeness may become a carte de visite at police stations, an illustration in the 'black book' of the Home Office, a photograph in the album... of the Discharged Prisoners' Aid Society, and a 'waxwork' figure, life size' at Madame Tussaud's. There is great importance attached to his appearance, and no less to his deeds, and their penalties.

Unusually for her time, although she absorbed some of the prevailing thinking about criminal heredity, Mrs Meredith did not see the women as the sum of their physical parts. She believed that by accepting God criminals had the potential for improvement in both body and soul. She certainly seemed to be achieving good results. The laundry was employing about two hundred women a year and attracting donations from across the country—but its success meant that it was in constant need of funds. By 1887 there were plans to sell Nine Elms House and move the laundry to 143 Clapham Road, just under a mile away.[42] The new location was on the site of the Marble Skating Rink, an iron building with a floor of polished white marble which had opened in 1876 and closed after only seven years of operation.[43]

I have not been able to find any images of the Marble Laundry, as it came to be known, but a description by Anne Beale was published in 1891 in the *Newbury House Magazine* ('for churchmen and churchwomen'). She wrote of its 'spacious buildings with high glazed roofs, and fitted with all the modern steam appliances'; there were also long ironing rooms and disinfecting troughs (the laundry was still taking in the washing of the sick). Beale also wrote of the ethos of the operation. The workers were a 'floating population' who might come and go, but no woman was turned away. Those unable to do laundry work were given plain needlework or sewed slippers for sale.[44]

The site was vast and accommodated Mrs Meredith' own home, where she lived with her sister, and the headquarters of all of Mrs Meredith's other organisations—the Addlestone Homes, a mission to Palestine and a charity sending out Christmas letters to thousands of prisoners across the world. The skating rink had earlier been converted

FIG.3 Dr Annie McCall's trailblazing work in south London, facilitated by Mrs Meredith, had an impact on the health of women worldwide.
A. McCall by Deneulain. Wellcome Library, 14909i

into a conference hall used by local organisations for mass meetings—a 'Divine Service for the People' held every Sunday at 11am with Sydney Gedge, a lay preacher, was typical.[45]

In 1885, before she moved the laundry, Mrs Meredith had started using the bar of the conference hall on the site to host a dispensary (outpatients clinic) for poor women and their children. To run it, she hired a newly qualified doctor from Manchester, Annie McCall (1859–1949) (*Fig.3*). She chose well. McCall went on to have an incalculable influence on the health outcomes of pregnant mothers in south London and on obstetrics practice worldwide. Although she and Mrs Meredith had many differences of opinion and parted ways in 1887 after eighteen months of collaboration they remained on good terms.[46] 'She was a woman of great parts,' wrote McCall. 'Her story is significant in the evolution of some of our more modern social attitudes, and I have no doubt that it will be embodied in other records of the times through which she passed.'

Mrs Meredith left a body of writing, numerous pamphlets and a handful of published books, all of it underpinned by her Christian ethos. Laundry is gruelling labour, requiring strength and skill, but she and her associates saw it not as punishment but as an opportunity for betterment, both moral and physical. For the women, it was time away from life on the streets, in some cases away from an abusive partner, with access to food, shelter and medical care. Mrs Meredith helped thousands of women and her efforts prevented many from reoffending and returning to prison. At one of the Mission's last annual meetings it was reported that in 1899 247 women had been received at the laundry on Clapham Road. Mr Justice Bruce, the chairman, made the point that 'Prison at the best, though of course punishment of the crime was absolutely necessary, was not a good reformatory, and it was well that other influences should be brought to bear on those who had the misfortune to be imprisoned.' He blamed alcoholism for much of the criminality of women and advocated treatment centres to help them.[47]

MRS MEREDITH DIED at Woburn Hill, Addlestone in October 1901, aged seventy-eight, leaving an estate of £1,200 to her sister Martha. She was buried at Brookwood Cemetery.[48] The Marble Laundry had already closed. Everything, the steam calendars, box mangles, hydro, engines, boilers, rotary washers, drying room fitters and ironing tables, was sold off at auction. A printworks was opened on the site two years later. It was more latterly the warehouse of Freeman's mail order catalogue and is now a complex of luxury flats. The Princess Mary Homes at Addlestone kept going, expanded its intake to older girls at risk of criminality and eventually became an approved school. It closed in 1981 with the land redeveloped for housing. The fate of Meredith's many charities is not clear.

Although there appears to be no collection of her papers, Mrs Meredith exists in the archives. You can find her in internet search engines, in newspaper collections, in scholarly books and listed in dusty tomes reporting on conferences and charities. In south London, where she did most of her work, however, there is little trace.[49]

The abolition of THE JURY OF MATRONS

WHEN THIRTY-SEVEN-YEAR-OLD Olive Wise arrived with her five children at the door of her local workhouse in Walthamstow, east London on the night of 3 December 1930 begging to be admitted, she was turned away. The next day she went to a neighbour with the body of her nine-month-old son in her arms. She had gassed him in the oven. Olive's trial took place the following month at the Old Bailey, where the jury convicted her of murder but recommended mercy. Mr Justice Charles agreed. He accepted her defence that she was a devoted mother driven to her terrible act by poverty and desperation. Her baby had been born out of wedlock after she had been abandoned by her husband. The baby's father was a widower who had promised marriage but only if she could prove that she was legally divorced.

It was obvious during her trial that Olive was pregnant again and her lawyer took the unusual step of requesting that a jury of matrons be convened to confirm it. This panel of twelve women concluded that Olive was indeed expecting a child (she was actually carrying twins) and, after this was confirmed by a doctor, the judge duly granted a stay of execution.[50]

What were the origins of this arcane legal process in which female members of the public, chosen because they happened to be in court at the time, decided whether a woman was pregnant or not and thereby

FIG.1 In John Gay's *The Beggar's Opera*, Filch the gaoler (carrying the keys) boasts of his sideline in impregnating women prisoners so that they can avoid the gallows. *William Hogarth (1697–1764), The Beggar's Opera (1729), Oil on canvas. Courtesy of Yale Center for British Art, Paul Mellon Collection, B1981.25.349*

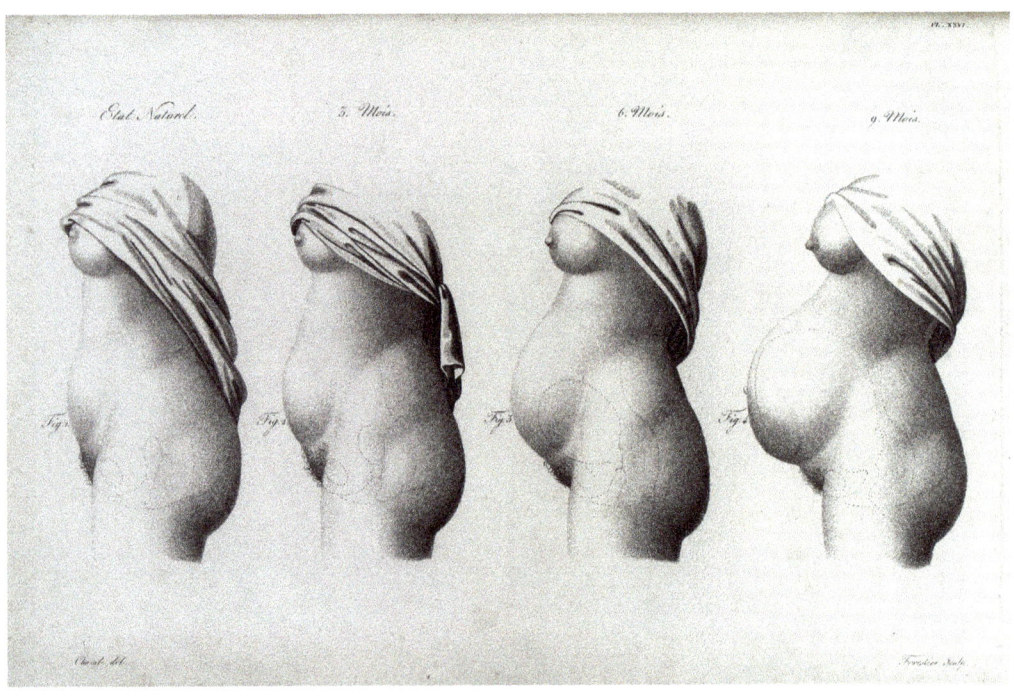

FIG.2 **The stages of pregnancy (1822).** *From 'Nouvelles démonstrations d'accouchements. Avec des planches en taille-douce, accompagnées d'un texte raisonné, propre à en faciliter l'explication Par J.-P. Maygrier'. Wellcome Collection*

affected the immediate fate of a condemned woman? They may lie in a thirteenth-century property dispute. In 1220 Peter Constable of Melton alleged that Muriel, the widow of his brother William, was falsely claiming to be pregnant by her husband. This was crucial to his fortunes. If there was no baby, Peter was the heir to his brother's estate. Muriel went through two examinations by 'matrons'–women who had had children–and stuck to her story, that is until forty-eight weeks after her last 'meeting' with her husband, at which point she dropped her claim and admitted that she had never been pregnant. She may have been planning to borrow another woman's baby to act the part of her own but was foiled when the court granted Peter the right to keep her in custody.[51]

The practice of convening a jury of matrons in court persisted for over seven hundred years. How did it finally come to an end? In this essay, I look at the long and troubling history of this post-conviction life-or-death plea and at some of the women whose lives depended on it.

THE PRACTICE OF convening a jury of matrons in order to determine whether a woman who has been sentenced to death and says she is pregnant is telling the truth features in Lucy Kirkwood's *The Welkin*,[52] which was first produced in London in 2020. The play is set in 1759 in rural Suffolk, where Sally Poppy is found guilty of a gruesome and senseless murder and is condemned to hang. In court, she 'pleads her belly', meaning that she claims to be pregnant. A pregnant woman could not be executed as this would effectively cause the death of the baby; capital punishment would have to wait until after she had given birth. There was a high chance, during that interval, that the authorities would commute her sentence. If, on the other hand, she was found not to be pregnant and she was not spared for other reasons, the sentence would usually be carried out within forty-eight hours. It is as well to remember that about ten per cent of capitally convicted men and women were executed, with the rest being transported, imprisoned, fined, sent into the military or to sea or, occasionally, pardoned.

But how could the court know whether a condemned prisoner claiming pregnancy was telling the truth? This is where the panel of twelve women, the jury of matrons, came in. Until 1919, when women were first permitted on court juries, their involvement was the only decision-making role assigned to women in any legal process. Men held all the offices of court, from the judge to the lowliest javelin bearer.

Who were the women on a jury of matrons? They were twelve married women with experience of child-bearing who were in court at the time of the trial. Typically, after a jury of matrons was convened, the under-sheriff of the court identified candidates who were then called to be empanelled. Sometimes women were reluctant to serve, perhaps because they knew the prisoner personally and wished not to be involved in her fate, or because they feared her. This was the case at York in 1809 at the murder trial of Mary Bateman, the so-called Yorkshire Witch. When Mary 'pleaded her belly' the women in the court stood up to leave and Justice Le Blanc had to order the court doors to be locked.[53]

A forematron was appointed and sworn in by the clerk of the court, followed by the other eleven members of the jury. There would have been occasions when not enough women were in the court building, so it is feasible that some jury members may have been women found passing by the court or even women living in the vicinity, fetched by the bailiff, as happens in *The Welkin*. The prisoner and the members of jury were then taken off to a private locked room. The bailiff was sworn to keep them 'without meat, drink or fire, candlelight excepted. You will suffer no person but the prisoner to speak to them; neither shall you speak to them yourself, unless it be to ask them if they are agreed on their verdict, without leave of the court.'[54]

LET'S NOW GO into that locked room, in which twelve matrons examine the capitally convicted prisoner. The early signs of pregnancy—tenderness of the breasts, waves of mild nausea, vivid dreams, for example—are sometimes experienced by the woman but are not apparent to anyone else. However, it was not the task of the matrons to assess whether the prisoner was merely pregnant. They had to decide whether she was 'quick with quick child'.

What does this strange phrase mean? 'Quick' derives from the Germanic and means alive. Quick with child means pregnant.[55] Quick with quick child means the pregnancy has progressed so far that the baby has moved in the womb, that it has 'quickened', producing a feeling of fluttering or tapping. Women who have already had a baby may experience stronger quickening earlier in their term—sometimes

FIG 3. 'Merry making on the Regent's birthday' by George Cruikshank (1812). A man and woman hang in the top right corner. *British Cartoon Prints. Collection (Library of Congress)*

as early as fourteen weeks—because the uterine muscles are more relaxed. The distinction between merely quick with child and quick with quick child arose because there was a belief that the foetus only received life at the point that it quickened. As the legal commentator William Blackstone said: 'Life... begins in contemplation of law as soon as an infant is able to stir in the mother's womb.'[56] The definition of quick with quick child was important in prosecutions for abortion, which was a felony crime and thus punishable by death.

There was also a little considered anomaly between the 'law of Nature' relating to quickening and the law of real property. In the latter, an infant was held to exist from the moment of its conception (as had been the case with Muriel in the thirteenth century) yet if a woman were found guilty of a hanging crime before her foetus had quickened it would be deemed not to exist and the foetus could be destroyed along with its mother.[57]

IF A WOMAN had good reason to believe that she would indeed be convicted and hanged, there were some strategies available to her. None guaranteed success. In London, where prisoners could languish for months before being called to court, it was not unknown for women of childbearing age to attempt to get pregnant while behind bars. In *The Beggar's Opera*, John Gay's 1728 portrait of the underbelly of London society, Filch has a notable line about such women.(*Fig.1*) He was paid, he said, to help 'the ladies to a pregnancy against their being called down to sentence'.

Some women played for time. In 1814 Justice Hardinge described Sarah Chandler's crime—counterfeiting bank notes—as 'the wickedest forgery ever perpetrated'. Sarah, who lived just outside Presteigne in Radnorshire, was kept so short of money for food and shoes for her children by her husband, a farmer, that she became desperate and resorted to making her own bank notes, or at least to making adjustments to real ones, at her kitchen table. Her scheme was creative and simple, if naïve. She hoodwinked a local printer into printing up the numbers '5' and '2' on sheets of paper and then cut them out and glued them over the '1' on notes from the local bank. She was soon arrested, tried, found guilty and given a sentence of death by Hardinge, who determined that she should hang, even though she was not part

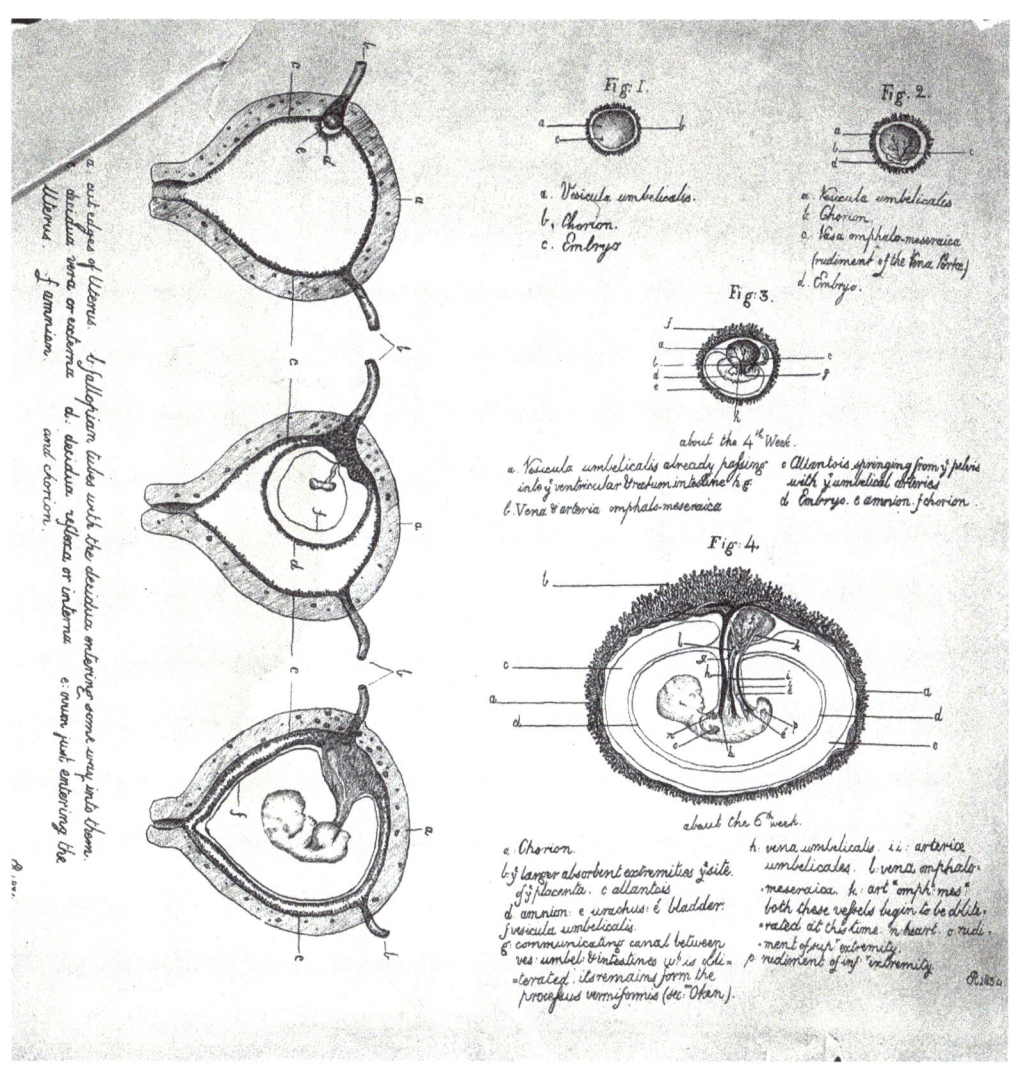

FIG.4 Development of the foetus in the uterus: seven figures, showing the embryo in the early stages of pregnancy. *Lithograph by C.R., c. 1834.* Wellcome Collection

of a counterfeiting gang, was caught early on and had no prior history of criminality. Sarah, although operating alone, had the misfortune to be part of a crime wave. The Bank Restriction Act of 1797, which for the first time allowed low denomination notes—£1 and £2—had led to an explosion of counterfeiting, which had an effect on the economy. Hardinge wanted to use Sarah's execution as an example to others and wrote to the Home Secretary, Lord Sidmouth, to dissuade him from recommending her for the Prince Regent's mercy: '[The] infliction of capital punishment upon Susanna [sic] Chandler is indispensable to public justice and mercy well understood.'

Sarah did not plead her belly at her trial, but soon afterwards her supporters, including directors of the bank whose notes she defaced, petitioned for leniency. When Hardinge received information from Sarah's friends suggesting that she was pregnant, he suspended the order for her execution, although he suspected that it was a scam. Still, he was prepared to wait in order to be absolutely sure and he was aware that there was strong local feeling about her.

Unluckily for Hardinge, the hiatus meant that Sarah, who was indeed not pregnant, escaped execution during the current assizes and would now have to wait for the next session of the court. This gave her friends enough time to organise her escape from prison: with their help she scaled the walls, disguised herself as a man and fled to Birmingham. By the time she was located two years later and hauled back to Presteigne, Hardinge had died and the will to kill her had evaporated. Sarah's sentence was commuted to transportation to New South Wales.[58]

ALTHOUGH MANY WOMEN had their deferred sentence of death commuted if they were pregnant at the time of their conviction, there were notable, and awful, exceptions to this. In 1757, Margaret Larney, a poor Irish woman, married with five children and living in the Covent Garden area of London, was arrested and charged with degrading the coin of the realm, an act of high treason.

Margaret—and possibly her husband too—earned money by filing off flakes of gold from the flat areas of gold sovereigns and selling them on to illicit dealers. At her trial at the Old Bailey Margaret claimed the witnesses were telling lies about her but that cut no ice with the jury and she was found guilty. Her husband was not convicted. Margaret claimed that she was pregnant and the jury of matrons agreed with her. While she was in Newgate Prison, she gave birth to a son but her pleas for the alternative punishment of transportation were not supported by Stephen Roe, the Ordinary (chaplain) of Newgate, who declared that her crimes were too serious to merit it. Margaret had 'contravened a law so important and necessary to the preservation of the current coin of the nation entire and undiminished, on which the public credit, commerce, national justice and the facility of dealing do greatly depend,' he said. Margaret was a Roman Catholic and Irish, which did not help her, and she refused to admit her guilt. The state liked condemned prisoners to be contrite as an example to others and as an affirmation that their death was justified. Margaret was strangled and then burnt at Tyburn on 2 October 1758. Larney was certainly unfortunate. Many others guilty of similar crimes were transported or imprisoned rather than executed. In 1781, at Kingston upon Thames, Ann Lucas was found guilty of coining silver, pleaded her belly and subsequently gave birth to twin sons. Then she was given a free pardon. The exact reason for her good fortune will never be known.[59]

By the end of the eighteenth century, it was generally only women convicted of murder who were left with little hope of mercy after giving birth and, of these, women who killed their husband were most at risk. In 1812 Edith Morrey and her husband George, farmers at Hankelow, just south of Crewe in Cheshire, who had five children, took on a new labourer, twenty-year-old John Lomas. Soon Edith, who was thirty-seven, was having an affair with him. One night the couple sneaked up on George while he was sleeping. Lomas attacked him with an axe while Edith held a candle and handed him a razor to finish the job. The couple were suspected immediately and both were charged with murder. Lomas was executed within days of their trial at Chester but Edith pleaded her belly. On 23 April 1813, four months after she gave birth to a son, she was drawn on a hurdle to the gallows and hanged for murder and petty treason, the crime of murdering your social superior, in this case her husband. Her body was donated to surgeons to be anatomised.[60]

AS MEDICAL SCIENCE advanced, so did nervousness over the accuracy of the jury of matrons' verdicts. By the early nineteenth century there were reports of surgeons and man-midwives being called in for their opinion. In 1804, Ann Hurle was facing death on the gallows for a £500 fraud—she had claimed an old man her aunt had worked for had signed shares over to her, which she then attempted to sell. When John Silvester, the Recorder of London (*see also pp.2–31*), asked her if she had anything to say as to why her sentence should not be carried out, her lawyer, answering on her behalf, said that she believed herself to be pregnant but was not sure. The jury of matrons was not sure either and after they declared that they could not make a decision, the sheriffs called in Dr Thynne who found that Ann was not quick with quick child and her execution outside Newgate proceeded.[61]

In 1833 Mary Wright, from a small village on the coast of Norfolk, was found guilty of murdering her husband by putting arsenic in his plum cakes. In court she pleaded her belly and was examined by a jury of matrons, whose verdict was that Mary was not quick with quick child. Justice Bolland was not convinced and because he wanted to be absolutely sure sent for not one surgeon but three. One of them, Arthur Crosse, disagreed with the matrons and declared that Mary was indeed pregnant. She later gave birth in prison and her sentence was commuted.[62]

A legal turning-point came in 1838, when the jury of matrons at the murder trial of Anne Wycherley in Stafford themselves requested the assistance of a surgeon. Justice Gurney's first reaction was to refuse: 'I think that I ought not, considering the terms of the bailiff's oath, to allow a surgeon to go to the room in which the jury of matrons is, and that they should come into court.' Eventually, Gurney agreed that Mr Greatorex, a surgeon and accoucheur (man-midwife) who happened to be married to the forematron of the jury and was in the courthouse because he was a witness in another case, could give evidence. He examined Ann and took the stand to say that he was of the opinion that Wycherley was not pregnant or, if she was, only in the early stages. The jury of matrons then retired and found that Wycherley was not pregnant.[63] Even then, the law was reluctant to proceed and Wycherley's sentence was stayed, but only for a few months. She was executed on 5 May outside the county gaol at Stafford.[64]

Doctors expressed horror at the thought that a mistake might be made in such cases. In 1843 the British Medical Association passed a resolution condemning the law that allowed a distinction between quick with child and quick with quick child and four years later there

FIG. 5 Anonymous broadside published around July 1879 commemorating the trial, sentence and execution of Kate Webster. *Wikimedia Commons*

was a stark example of the need for caution. A jury of matrons, who had earlier been offered the services of a surgeon but declined it, declared Mary Ann Hunt, who had been found guilty of murder, not pregnant. The Home Secretary ordered an examination by doctors who decided she was. Three months later she gave birth to a premature son.[65]

AFTER THE 1930s pleading the belly was rare. It always caused a scene when it cropped up in court. Even allowing for the journalist's dramatic licence and casual misogyny, *The Globe* reporter's account of the awful events at the Old Bailey on 8 January 1872 retains its power to shock. When Christiana Edmunds, the so-called 'Chocolate Cream Killer', was found guilty of poisoning confectionery with strychnine, which had resulted in at least one death, as the judge passed sentence he struggled to contain his emotions. Then the Clerk of Arraigns asked Edmunds whether she was pregnant:

> The prisoner... whispered to the female warder, who again whispered to the jailer, who said aloud, 'She says she is, my lord.' There was a profound sensation among the bystanders at the unexpected announcement which was not diminished when the words, 'Let the Sheriff empanel a jury of matrons forthwith,' were heard... After about twenty minutes a dozen well-to-do and respectably-dressed women—who could have supposed that a dozen such were to be found in such a place?—were captured and directed to enter the jury-box, into which they marched and took their seats as if it was a matter of everyday occurrence.

> Mrs Adelaide Whittaw, the forewoman, was sworn separately, and then the rest in a body. It was arranged that they should see the prisoner in the Sheriff's parlour. Half an hour elapsed when a messenger came into Court, and an inquiry was made aloud by the Judge whether there was an accoucheur in Court. Presently a doctor was found, and directed to join the matrons. Half an hour more of suspense and eager interest. A messenger again comes in and whispers, and the rumour goes about that the doctor requires a stethoscope. There is a touch of comedy even in the midst of the tragic scene, for they say that a policeman has been sent to fetch one, but has brought back a telescope instead. More delay,

more suspense. Here they are at last. The prisoner again at the bar, the matrons again in the box. The verdict is spoken by the forewoman in a single word 'Not.'

The humanity of the rule of law which leaves this delicate matter to the decision of twelve women accidentally present in court during a murder trial [...] is [...] very questionable, and the result has on more than one occasion proved to be very fallible. The sort of women who care to be present at such scenes are not presumably the most intelligent or best educated of the community, and the question which they have to investigate might in modern days of medical science be answered far more satisfactorily by a medical man. Besides, the question itself is somewhat difficult, even for medical men to answer, and one about which there has been much professional disputation in modern times.

The Globe's writer then recalled the near-misses in the pregnancy verdicts on Mary Wright in 1832 and on Mary Ann Hunt in 1847 and expressed the hope that the matrons would soon be replaced with 'proper scientific investigation'.[66] Edmunds' sentence was commuted to life imprisonment and she spent the rest of her life in Broadmoor Criminal Lunatic Asylum.

When Kate Webster (*Fig.5*), who committed a particularly grisly murder, made her plea for a stay of execution in 1879, the judge, Mr Justice Denman, observed that this was his first experience of the kind in thirty-two years on the bench.[67] The editors of *The Lancet* were incensed by the process: 'The whole episode of "a jury of matrons" is a farce which justice, indecorously and at an unseemly time, performs for the gratification of archæological tastes.'[68]

Further cases sporadically troubled the media, serving only to provide evidence of the pointlessness of convening a jury of matrons when doctors would also give evidence and of subjecting pregnant women to a death sentence only to commute it later. Carrie Thomas, a destitute, unmarried servant who had been in and out of the workhouse, was condemned at Bodmin in 1906 for drowning her child (she said she had intended to drown herself too but could not manage it) and respited by the judge, but within days had given birth to a premature child who died. At the inquest for the baby, the medical officer of Bodmin prison told a coroner's court that Thomas had not been fit to stand trial.[69]

There was also a growing understanding of how women's difficult lives affected their mental health. In 1913 twenty-six-year-old married nurse Ada Annie Williams was convicted, while pregnant, of the murder of her four-year-old disabled son, who had been born out of wedlock. Her husband, with whom she had two further children, had constantly taunted her about him, deserted her and failed to pay adequate maintenance.[70] She gave birth to a boy in Holloway Prison and was discharged on licence in 1921. In 1917, twenty-five-year-old munitions worker Ethel Stevens was convicted of drowning her baby son at Stanwell in Surrey and sentenced to death but claimed pregnancy and was respited.

In January 1931 change finally came with Olive Wise's trial for killing her baby son. Later that year the jury of matrons was abolished after Parliament passed the Sentence of Death (Expectant Mothers) Act, presented by Labour MP Edith Picton-Turbervill (*Fig.6*). The legislation also stated that women who are capitally convicted while pregnant must automatically have their sentences commuted.

What happened to Olive? She was released from prison in July 1932, having served seventeen months, an apt illustration of the inappropriateness of her original sentence. She married the father of her twins and the boy she had killed.[71] In 2022, having seen the article on my website, one of Olive's granddaughters wrote to tell me that her father had been among the four boys taken into care by Dr Barnado's and that the twins Olive had given birth to were alive and well. Many of Olive's descendants had gone on to do well in life.

Although the jury of matrons has gone, pregnancy is still a plea in capital cases. In 2016 in Vietnam Nguyen Thi Hue, aged forty-two, who had been convicted of drug offences and sentenced to die, arranged for a male prisoner to smuggle his sperm to her. Her subsequent pregnancy protected her from the firing squad and her sentence was commuted to life imprisonment.[72]

FIG.6 In 1930 the Labour MP Edith Picton-Turbervill sponsored a bill to abolish the jury of matrons and automatically commute the death sentences of pregnant women. *Via LSE Library (Wikimedia Commons)*

Cartes de Visite of WORKING WOMEN

WHAT IS A *carte de visite*? A small monochrome photograph, usually a portrait but sometimes a scene, printed on thin paper and pasted onto board, very popular in the latter part of the nineteenth century. You can fit one in the palm of your hand. Of course, they are more than this. They carry identity and meaning and they offer insights into worlds long vanished.

Cartes de visite were highly exchangeable and indeed were handed out to friends, family and perhaps employers, both past and potential, as an *aide-memoire*. They could be kept in albums or not. They are stackable, like a deck of cards. If you browse lists of them on eBay, as I have done, you will see that they depict all sorts: women in crinoline dresses, peers of the realm, married couples, labourers in caps and aprons, Victoria and Albert surrounded by their royal brood, dapper young men with or without their top hats. Subjects could choose to pose standing, seated, lounging on a chaise-longue, holding a lapdog, against a fancy painted background, on a swirly carpet, with a *papier mâché* urn, next to a balustrade, or without any of those accoutrements, utterly plain, as if to say 'here you see the essence of me'.

The *carte de visite* appeared on the market after 1851 when Frederick Scott Archer (1813–1857), a sculptor, published his new system of

FIG.1 The photographer Disdéri looking through an album of his *cartes de visite* (c. 1860). *Courtesy of Musée Carnavalet, Paris*

photography in which a negative was created on a glass plate coated with collodion.[73] The process had the edge over daguerrotypes, which were one-offs and could not be reproduced, and over calotypes because multiple paper copies of collodion prints could be created and were sharper and clearer. Unlike the systems developed by Louis Daguerre and William Henry Fox Talbot, Archer's invention was unpatented, and thus did not require practitioners to purchase a licence to use it. It revolutionised photography, opening up what had been an expensive genteel hobby to anyone who could afford to set up with a camera, props and premises.

Three years after Archer published his article, Paris photographer André-Adolphe-Eugène Disdéri (*Fig.1*) patented the *carte de visite* format. He constructed a camera with several lenses, enabling him to take multiple exposures. Then he cut the resulting print into rectangles and glued each one onto a sheet of thin cardboard. This new way of commissioning a portrait had universal appeal, among the famous and important as well as the hoi-polloi. However, legend has it that the process did not become popular until Emperor Napoleon III visited Disdéri's studio in 1859. Images of celebrities, politicians, entertainers and criminals became highly collectable items, traded like cigarette cards or, more recently, Pokémon cards.

My interest in this early form of 'selfie' was ignited when I started researching a domestic servant who in 1872 had fled post-Commune Paris for London and was convicted of a serious crime a few months later. I came across two *cartes de visite* of her. One was taken in a photographer's studio, possibly in Paris. She stands holding on to a chair and wears a skirt with a white blouse and a servant's cap and looks happy and relaxed. The other, made by Eugène Appert, shows her from the bust up and wearing a revealing dress. The overall impression is that she is bloated and louche. When I looked closely at the two images, I noticed that the first had been used to create the second, which was a photomontage. Her cap had been sliced off and her head cut out and stuck on someone else's torso. It was an attempt to manipulate her public image, to her detriment, and it was made for sale and profit. Appert was facing financial ruin at the time.

Appert had a history of using photomontage for political purposes. After the Commune fell, when thousands of its supporters were detained by the government, he obtained a licence—at considerable expense—to

CARTES DE VISITE

FIG.2 Photomontage of Chantiers women's prison at Versailles by Eugène Appert (1871). Louise Michel is third from the right, arms crossed.
Courtesy of Musée Carnavalet, Paris

visit the prisons to photograph them. Many of these desperate people leapt at the opportunity to be photographed and called on their relatives to bring in clean clothes. They had been living in very difficult conditions and relished the chance to show that they were decent, respectable people. Some of the prisoners may have felt that if they were executed or exiled to the French colonies in the Pacific, as many were, their families would at least have something to remember them by.

The process was simple. Appert arrived at the prison with an assistant. They set up their equipment in the yard, pinned up a plain sheet on the prison wall and placed a chair in front. As an inducement Appert offered his subjects unlimited copies of the resulting *cartes*. The photographs, many of which have survived in collections and archives, show the prisoners in various poses. Some look defiant, others defeated. At Chantiers, the women's prison in Versailles, a few are photographed in profile, drinking from beer bottles or smoking. One has her foot on the chair. No doubt, for these women, the episode was a welcome diversion from the rigours of incarceration under a brutal and abusive regime, and Appert would have done nothing to encourage more decorous poses. For her photograph, Louise Michel, the defiant socialist activist, sits armed crossed, unsmiling (*see Fig.2 and p.101*).

What Appert did not tell the prisoners was that he planned to use the images to create 'fake news' propaganda. In his studio, he photographed actors wearing the appropriate uniforms and clothes of both the protagonists and the victims of notorious atrocities that occurred during the Commune, and he also photographed the locations of the events. To make his photomontage, he cut out the bodies of the actors and stuck them on the background, adding the heads or upper bodies of the prisoners. *Et voilà!* He had fabricated an image that looked as if it was a true record. The montages, which he marketed as 'Atrocities of the Commune', sold in their thousands. The women of the prison at Chantiers would have been bemused to see their heads on other people's bodies. Although they are not shown taking part in crimes, the general impression of them is one of degeneracy.

For a while, Appert must have thought that his fortune was made. It was not. His *cartes* were widely and illegally copied, and in December 1871, with most of the post-Commune trials over, in an effort to 'move on', the government banned the sale of images of the Commune. Appert's investment went down the drain. By the time he manipulated the image

CARTES DE VISITE

FIG. 3 Eliza Jane Birch (later Shaw) was nurse to Selina Causton, the wife of a businessman and Liberal MP

of my poor servant whose life imploded in London and who fled back to Paris, he was involved in an expensive lawsuit and deeply in debt. He must have thought he could profit, at least a little, from exploiting this woman's notoriety.

While I was researching this topic, which was totally new to me, I came to the conclusion that I needed to understand better the medium of *cartes de visite* and how working women used them. I wanted to understand what prompted women to have their photograph taken, and what they might expect to get from it. Was it unusual for a woman on a low wage to commission a photograph, or was it was something an employer would have paid for? I decided to buy some *cartes de visite* of women to see if they could yield answers.

Although they were cheap—none cost me more than £8—I could see at once that they are small objects of desire, treasured as much by their original owners as the dealers who had sold them to me. They arrived tenderly wrapped, sometimes twice. Each time, I felt a strange and strong elation. They were personal and intimate, and also enigmatic. They captured a fleeting pulse of a person's life; they could not indicate more than a momentary facial expression and therefore they were not a measure of character or personality.

Did they answer my questions? Not really, but I present them here, each with a few facts where these have been revealed with research, and some commentary. They have none of Appert's tricksiness, but they are nevertheless replete with interesting information. All of them turned out to be not quite what I had assumed.

SOMEONE HAD WRITTEN her name, on the back of her carte (*Fig.3*), so 'Eliza Jane Birch' and 'ditto ditto Shaw' was easy enough to find in the 1881 census, but almost every assumption I made about Eliza was proved wrong.

She wears a white apron, cuffs and headgear so I thought she was a maid. Not true. Eliza was a nurse. In 1881, along with a ladies' maid, she was staying at the Royal Bath Hotel in Bournemouth, Dorset, both of them employees of Richard Causton, a wholesale stationer and Liberal MP for Colchester, and his wife Selina.[74] The hotel, a giant white confection of turrets and pediments, was built to accommodate the growing popularity of sea-swimming as a health treatment. At

CARTES DE VISITE

FIG.4 Unknown woman, photographed by Herbert Hole of Williton and Minehead

the time Eliza and the Caustons were there, it had just reopened after an extensive refurbishment.[75] Why the Caustons chose to come to Bournemouth we will probably never know. They were childless after ten years of marriage so perhaps they were looking for a cure and Eliza was part of that, but this is pure speculation on my part.

Four years after the visit to Bournemouth, Eliza married Samuel Shaw, a draper whose business was based in Stoke Newington, north London. He was not as lowly as he might sound. The marriage certificate has his father down as a 'gentleman', meaning that he did not work for a living, and Eliza was also from solid stock—her father was a Registrar of Births and Deaths. By the time of the 1901 census Samuel, still in his forties, had retired from his business and ten years later he and Eliza had moved to a nine-room house in leafy Chertsey in Surrey. They must have been doing well.

Let's return to the *carte* itself. It is undated, but Eliza looks as if she is in her twenties, so it may have been made while she was working for the Caustons, that is, before she married; afterwards she would be unlikely to work outside the home. The person who wrote her name so carefully, if not Eliza herself, would probably have known her in both her single and married states. Perhaps this *carte* was in the possession of her former employer, Selina Causton. The back of the *carte* shows that it was made by Alfred Hugh Harman at 79 High Street, Peckham, a suburb of southeast London. Richard Causton was for many years an MP for the neighbouring constituency of Southwark (he became Baron Southwark in 1910), so perhaps the Caustons lived near Peckham and Eliza lived with them.[76] Alfred Harman was born in Camberwell in 1841. He advertised himself as an 'artist photographer'—hence the palette and brushes on the reverse of the *carte*. In 1878, while still based in Peckham, he patented a method for producing enlarged photographs 'with an artistic finish' and a year later began using a new process, gelatine dry plates, at his new business, Britannia Works Company, in Cranbrook Road, in Ilford, Essex. In 1902 the company carried the Ilford name, which went on to become one of the most recognisable camera film brands in the world.[77]

THE NEXT IN my series is quite different—an older woman, unnamed, wearing a dark wrinkled dress, waist apron, a coarse woven shawl, white

CARTES DE VISITE

FIG.5 'Sarah', wearing a good dress and pearl earrings, photographed by Charles Cross of Bow in east London

cap and boots (*Fig.4*). She rests one hand on a chair, and there are some drapes to the right. A degree of solemnity was required when having one's photograph made—it was not considered seemly to smile or laugh—but even so she looks careworn and long-suffering, although she may simply have had a difficult day. Again, I at first assumed she was a servant, but many women wore aprons as part of their normal domestic attire, so that is not necessarily the case. The background is a plain wall. Is that a stain to the left of the drape? This could be a house rather than a studio, but it is impossible to be sure. For all we know, this could be the photographer Herbert Henry Hole's mother.

The verso of the *carte* bears his imprint: Hole of Williton and Minehead. He was born in 1837 at Crowcombe in Somerset. Like many photographers he started off as a printer but by 1871, at the height of the fashion for CDVs, he was describing himself as a 'printer and photographer'. When he made this *carte* he had studios in two towns.

Altogether, this is the most unsophisticated of the five *cartes*. The accoutrements—the chair, the drape—look real, quite unlike the *papier mâché* artifice used in many *cartes*, but the paper is thin and flimsy. I don't want to speculate that its relative crudeness arises because it was made in a small rural town in the West Country, but I can't dismiss the idea completely.

JUDGING BY SARAH'S leg-of-mutton sleeves, I would date her *carte de visite* (*Fig.5*) to the 1890s. There is a tantalising clue on the back: 'Mrs J. C. Wright from Sarah' appears in ink in a somewhat unconfident hand. I have been trying to think of some scenarios behind the words. Did Sarah, if she is the subject of the card, hand it to Mrs Wright as if to say, 'Remember me from our interview and please hire me?' If so, why did she not write her full name? 'Sarah' implies intimacy. Perhaps Sarah gave it as a memento on leaving Mrs Wright's service.

What else can we learn from the photograph? Domestic service was generally a young person's occupation, not often compatible with the married state. Sarah looks middle-aged, and so is likely to have been single. Women servants' starched accessories became frillier the further up the domestic hierarchy they went. My first thought was that because she is not in the first flush of youth Sarah may have been quite senior in a household, but counter to that, her apron is plain. Plain aprons

FIG.6 A servant reading photographed by Arthur Melhuish—but is this a genuine portrait or a an advertising gimmick?

were for scullerymaids, for those who did the most work and would get the most dirty; fancy ones were for housekeepers. Sarah, with her earrings and good dress, does not look like a scullery maid, so perhaps she worked in a household where she was the only servant or one of only a few, or perhaps she worked in a business such as a hotel or restaurant.

I have not been able to trace Mrs J. C. Wright—it's too common a name—and the location of the photographer is of no help. Sarah may have lived near Charles Cross's shop and studio at 114 Campbell Road in Bow, east London, but Mrs Wright could have lived anywhere.

The photographer himself, on the other hand, was easy to find. Charles Cross, born in Bow, was the son of a blacksmith. He had the studio from at least 1891 to 1901 but by 1911 had given it up to become a publican—he ran the Wilson's Arms further down Campbell Road, at No. 29.

A MAID SITTING down and reading (*Fig.6*). Oh my word! Servants caught with their noses in novels were liable to be sacked on the spot. Women, as the weaker sex, apparently, were susceptible to moral corrosion via fictional stories. Although by the end of the nineteenth century it was certainly deemed helpful to have a maid who could read the words on everyday products (see the first essay in this collection, in which Eliza Fenning came to grief in 1815 for her ability to do exactly that), the only acceptable reading material was the Bible, a prayer book, or a guide to running the employer's household. It makes me wonder what kind of family would tolerate the unusual behaviour of the woman in this *carte de visite*.

It was not unusual for a woman to pose with a book in hand, just as Anastasia Ingleton did (*Fig.7*), although it was rare to see a photograph of a woman so absorbed in the words on the page. It almost resembles a painting—women reading was a subject many artists, most of them male, tackled. Some of them found this activity an erotic moment. Reading women, almost always of the educated classes and some of them disturbingly young, were painted languishing on chaises longues, their deranged clothes verging on *semi-deshabillée*. The implication is that they had let their guard down, rendering them open to suggestion.

It makes me wonder whether the woman shown in the *carte* was really a maidservant. I have my doubts. She looks like an actress

CARTES DE VISITE

FIG.7 Anastasia Ingleton, photographed by A&G Taylor, worked as a governess

playing a part, perhaps created to advertise the photographer's skill or to catch a customer's eye. Genre *cartes de visite*, in which a scene is set up with characters played by actors, were a notable section of the market. Indeed, actors would have themselves photographed in costume as their most popular characters. There were also humorous scenes with captions, precursors of seaside postcards ('Why don't yer mother cut yer hair?' complains a blind grandmother, mistaking a donkey for her grandson); religious scenes (a young boy prays fervently by his bed); love scenes (a smock-wearing milkman steals a kiss from a pretty maidservant); and, of course, plenty of under-the-counter porn. I can't say that the photographer was involved in anything of that nature. Indeed, it is quite unlikely. The verso is stamped with the credentials of Arthur James Melhuish (1829–1895), 'portrait-painter and photographer', a respectable religious nonconformist with royal patronage—he photographed Queen Victoria and produced a notable volume of photographs of Windsor Castle.

The woman's cap is of a style that makes me think the photograph was taken at the end of the nineteenth century or possibly the beginning of the twentieth, so this *carte de visite* may have been made by one of Melhuish's children. In the 1891 census, four unmarried daughters and a son, all in their thirties and all described as artist-photographers, were living with their parents. By this time the family had moved from their home near Portman Square in central London to Belsize Park, in Hampstead. With them lived Amy E. Leigh, aged nineteen, a general servant. Could our maid be Amy? Ten years later she was listed in the census as a dressmaker so perhaps she sewed her own frilly apron and sat for a genre card at the request of her employers.

THE FINAL CARTE in this little series bears a name, Anastasia Ingleton, and a date (*Fig.7*). The 1871 census tells me that twenty-one-year-old Anastasia Ingleton, the daughter of a twice-widowed West Ham butcher, was working as a governess, so she may have still been one six years later when she went to a studio in Fenchurch Street to have her photograph taken. Anastasia is in full fig. Her two-piece outfit features a fitted jacket and separate skirt with some horizontal draping and ruffles, trimmed with velvet ribbon. The skirt is gathered into a bustle at the back, possibly with some sort of mini-crinoline to support it. As I sit at my desk in my yoga pants and T-shirt I feel both admiration and pity for her. How did Anastasia manage to go to the toilet without mishap? It was perfectly possible (collapsible bustles and split pantalettes), as I have learned through watching it demonstrated on a YouTube video of a woman in nineteenth-century garb.

A governess was certainly a domestic servant but not one doing manual work. Anyone who has read *Jane Eyre* will know about the awkward inbetween space into which the governess falls: not good enough to socialise with the family, too lah-di-dah to make friends in the servants' kitchen. Perhaps things were not so for Anastasia. She may have been employed in a middle-class family rather than landed gentry as Jane Eyre was, and if so it was likely to have been a nonconformist one, or at least a family that was comfortable with Anastasia's low-church beliefs. How do we know what these were? In 1881 she married Stephen Smoothy, a minister in the Congregationalist Church. They went on to have five children and lived for many years in Fulbourn, Cambridgeshire. In the photo, she holds a book which is probably a Bible.

The photographer was A&G (Andrew and George) Taylor, Aberdonian brothers who built their business from the 1860s and claimed theirs was 'the biggest photographers in the world'. In 1886 they had thirty-six branches throughout the United Kingdom and six in the United States, so perhaps they were.

CARTES DE VISITE democratised portraiture. For the first time, an image of oneself was within the reach of almost everyone. They were highly collectable: royalty, celebrities and criminals were collected and inserted into albums. They were also useful as political propaganda, manipulating emotions with manufactured scenarios. But by 1871, when Appert was making his photomontages, they were already on the way out, superseded by the larger format cabinet cards.

Why did they decline and disappear? Fashion and technological advances probably. But perhaps they never really went away—traces of them persist in the form of cigarette cards, postcards and in profile pictures on social media.

TRIAL by COMBAT
The opening night of the ROYAL COBURG

ON WHIT MONDAY 1818, 11 May, *The Morning Advertiser* carried an advertisement for that night's inaugural show at the Royal Coburg (today known as the Old Vic), a brand new theatre in Lambeth Marsh on the south side of the Thames. After a short address by Mr Munro to mark the opening of the theatre, the main offering was to be the premiere of a new William Barrymore[78] melodrama, *Trial by Battle; or, Heaven Defend the Right*, followed by a 'Grand Asiatic Ballet' *Alzora and Nerine, or The Fairy Gift,* performed by Mr LeClercq and his wife, and featuring his children and pupils, and closing with the 'splendid harlequinade' *Midnight Revelry,* based on Milton's *Comus*, which included 'new and extensive scenery, machinery mechanical changes, tricks and metamorphoses'.

It was an evening designed to please everyone, to tempt City-dwellers to venture across the new Waterloo Bridge and on to the far-from-respectable Surrey shore. Although the Coburg had an advantage over other south London venues, being so close to the new bridge, there was still some reluctance to venture across to the 'wrong' side of the Thames.

Trial by Battle was nothing if not topical. It must have been in preparation while the court case that inspired it was still playing out back over the bridge in the Court of King's Bench at Westminster Hall. The

THE OPENING NIGHT OF THE ROYAL COBURG

FIG.1 'The last scene of Trial by Battle' shows the interior of the Royal Coburg, with Geralda (centre front) looking appealingly out of the frame and a cast of medieval-style soldiers on stage, Baron Falconbridge and the honourable smuggler Henrie facing each other off on either side of an adjudicator. An orange seller in yellow is to the right; she may not have predicted the use to which the oranges were put. *From R. Wilkinson, (1819). Londina Illustrata. Vol. 2. London: Robert Wilkinson*

FIG. 2 & 3 Mary Ashford encountered Abraham Thornton at a dance in Erdington on Whit Monday 1817. *Author's collection and Wellcome Collection*

trial, which had attracted the horrified fascination of people of all ranks of society, was unique. The accused was Abraham Thornton (*Fig.3*), widely held to have got away with the rape and murder of Mary Ashford (*Fig. 2*) when he was tried at Warwick the previous summer. Now he was being prosecuted for the murder again, but this time the trial was a civil case, brought by the victim's brother. It nevertheless carried the death penalty. The case was notorious, the talk of parlours and drawing-rooms the length and breadth of the country, and the scenes outside the courtroom were messy. Every time Thornton made the journey from King's Bench Prison in Newington to the Court of King's Bench sitting at Westminster Hall, crowds of onlookers jostled to catch sight of him, hiss or boo him, or better still, to bag a place in court to watch the legal drama unfold.

Almost exactly a year before the Royal Coburg opened, on the night of 26 May, which was also Whit Monday, twenty-year-old Mary Ashford, left a party in an inn near Erdington, on the outskirts of Birmingham, in the company of two friends and Thornton, a beefy twenty-five-year-old bricklayer from nearby Castle Bromwich. He had suddenly latched onto her and her friends at the end of the evening and insisted on walking with them. Mary and her friends parted during the early hours, leaving her alone with Thornton. Early the next morning her bruised and bloody body was found drowned in a stagnant pond on her route home.

Immediately identified as the prime suspect, Thornton admitted to having had sex with Mary but not to murdering her. Before the trial at Warwick Assizes in August, his canny solicitor had prepared the ground by propagating the theory that Mary had thrown herself in the pond out of a sense of shame for her regrettable lapse in behaviour. The judge made it clear that he thought Mary had consented to sex after Thornton had used 'great importunity' to persuade her to give in and that if there had not been a rape Thornton had no motive to kill her, because the only reason for doing that would have been to achieve her silence.

Thornton's acquittal surprised and outraged Mary's friends and supporters. Sponsored by the magistrate who had originally investigated the crime, Mary's brother William sued Thornton using 'Appeal of Murder', a civil suit of medieval origin designed to give families a means of avenging a death. Thornton was arrested and taken to London but he was a singular character, seemingly unfazed by this latest development and coolly confident that he would be acquitted for a second time.

FIG.3 The Royal Coburg in 1820, renamed the Royal Victoria Theatre in 1833, and nicknamed the Old Vic. *Author's collection*

THE OPENING NIGHT OF THE ROYAL COBURG

The Westminster Hall case was heard by four judges. After several hearings, Thornton, advised by his smart barristers, countered William Ashford's suit with his own dramatic challenge. On 17 November, after being charged at the bar, he threw down a white leather gauntlet and declared his right to 'trial by battel', that is, he and William Ashford would slug it out hand-to-hand, to the death of one of them, with cudgels and shields in Smithfield, the cattle market.

This provoked much consternation, not least among the judges. After much deliberation over whether trial by battle was still a legal process, they reluctantly admitted that it was and that the burly bricklayer was free to proceed. The problem for his opponent, William Ashford, was that he was a slightly-built lad of twenty-three. Thornton would swat him like a fly. Ashford was forced to withdraw and Thornton walked free from the courtroom. Public disapproval was so severe, however, that he eventually took himself off to America.[79]

ALTHOUGH THE DESIGN of the new theatre was plain with a simple classical façade, it was ambitious—costs ran to a massive £12,000—and boasted state-of-the-art scene-painting and property rooms, as well as an in-house gas-making plant and gasometer. The project itself was the brainchild of Daniel Dunn and James King, the lessees of the Royal Surrey on Blackfriars Road, who in 1816 had not been able to meet the rent on that site and decided instead to build a new theatre.

Among the investors were the Waterloo Bridge Company and John Thomas Serres, once a marine painter to George III.[80] Serres supplied works for the Coburg's ornate Grand Marine Saloon, which was in the area now occupied by the foyer. His subjects included 'Neptune in a Coach drawn by Sea Horses', 'The Bombardment of Algiers' and portraits of Princess Charlotte and Prince Leopold—all now lost—and he had helpfully used what remained of his influence with the Royal family to obtain the patronage of the daughter of the Prince of Wales, Princess Charlotte, and her husband Prince Leopold of Saxe-Coburg, after whom the theatre was named. Another saloon in the basement was lit with gas and lined with gilt caryatids supporting the roof and casts from the ancient world.

The theatre had been a difficult build from the start. It was not just that the theatre was located on the south bank of the Thames.

It was also resting on marshland; its foundations were reinforced using rubble from the north bank's old Savoy Palace, which had been demolished to make way for Waterloo Bridge itself. Investment in the theatre was slow and this led to delays. It wasn't helped in 1817 by a strike of construction workers who walked out protesting that they had not been paid. The project was saved at the eleventh hour with a large cash injection from Joseph Glossop, the son of a wealthy local tallow chandler, who bought out the other investors and appointed himself theatre manager.

The Coburg opened on 11 May 1818 in an 'unfinished state'.[81] Even so, it must have been a night to remember. The building was built to accommodate an audience of 3,800 and the orchestra pit up to thirty performers. Gas-powered cut-glass lustres shone over and on either side of the stage, while blue and gold boxes and gilt pillars shimmered. This description is from *The Gentleman's Magazine*:

> There are two tiers of boxes. These, as well as the whole interior of the theatre, are painted a fawn colour, ornamented with gold wreaths of flowers, and in the centre of each box is an allegorical painting. The pit and gallery are so constructed, that every part of the stage (which is very spacious) may be viewed from them. The drop scene is a view of Claremont [Princess Charlotte's residence].[82]

Tickets started at 1 shilling for the gallery, increasing to two shillings for the pit (seated with backless benches) and three and four shillings for the upper and lower boxes. At 8 o'clock they were reduced to half price.

Everyone who attended the opening night of the Coburg would have been aware of the absence of one of its patrons: Princess Charlotte. The twenty-one-year-old heir to the throne was widely admired for her strength of character and for being neither corrupt like her father, the Prince Regent, nor foolish like her mother, Princess Caroline. With her husband Prince Leopold of Saxe-Coburg, Charlotte had laid a foundation stone at the northwest corner of the Royal Coburg site in September 1816 but she died fourteen months later, a few days after delivering a stillborn son. As the theatre audience for *Trial by Battle* walked through the refreshment room where they would have seen her portrait they perhaps reflected for a moment on the fragility of life.

FIG.4 Waterloo Bridge, looking west, with part of Somerset House (1817). The Royal Coburg is not in view. *Robert Havell aft. Thomas S. Roberts. Yale Center for British Art, Paul Mellon Collection*

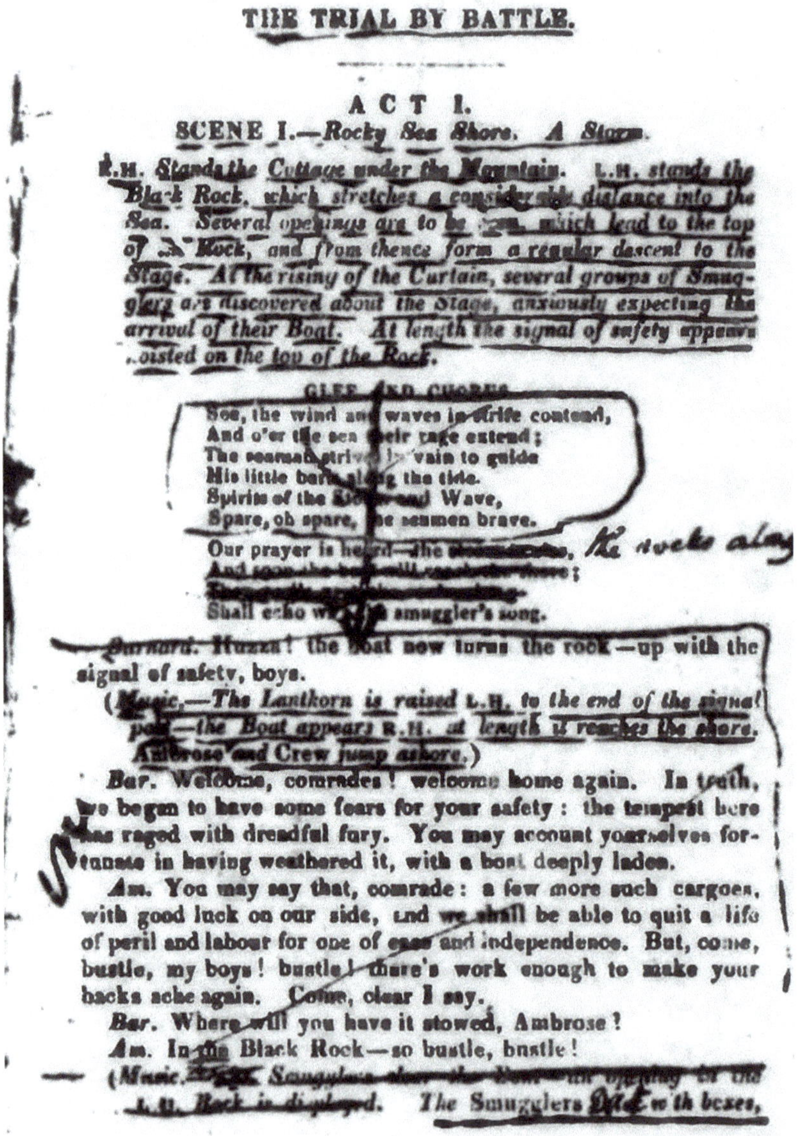

THE TRIAL BY BATTLE.

ACT I.
SCENE I.—*Rocky Sea Shore. A Storm.*

R.H. Stands the Cottage under the Mountain. L.H. stands the Black Rock, which stretches a considerable distance into the Sea. Several openings are to be seen, which lead to the top of the Rock, and from thence form a regular descent to the Stage. At the rising of the Curtain, several groups of Smugglers are discovered about the Stage, anxiously expecting the arrival of their Boat. At length the signal of safety appears hoisted on the top of the Rock.

GLEE AND CHORUS.

See, the wind and waves in strife contend,
And o'er the sea their rage extend;
The seaman strives in vain to guide
His little bark along the tide.
Spirits of the Storm and Wave,
Spare, oh spare, the seamen brave.
Our prayer is heard—the clouds are gone,
And soon the boat will reach the shore;
The tempest's fury now is o'er,
Shall echo with the smuggler's song.

Barnard. Huzza! the boat now turns the rock—up with the signal of safety, boys.

(*Music.*—The Lanthorn is raised L.H. to the end of the signal post.—the Boat appears R.H. at length it reaches the shore. *Ambrose and Crew jump ashore.*)

Bar. Welcome, comrades! welcome home again. In truth, we began to have some fears for your safety: the tempest here has raged with dreadful fury. You may account yourselves fortunate in having weathered it, with a boat deeply laden.

Am. You may say that, comrade: a few more such cargoes, with good luck on our side, and we shall be able to quit a life of peril and labour for one of ease and independence. But, come, bustle, my boys! bustle! there's work enough to make your backs ache again. Come, clear I say.

Bar. Where will you have it stowed, Ambrose?

Am. In the Black Rock—so bustle, bustle!

(*Music.*—Smugglers enter the Boat—an opening in the L.H. Rock is displayed. The Smugglers file off with boxes,

FIG.5 A page from William Barrymore's *Trial by Battle, or Heaven Defend the Right: A Melodramatic Spectacle*, with the director's amendments.
Date of handwritten amendments unknown

THE OPENING NIGHT OF THE ROYAL COBURG

THIS WAS THE background to the performance of William Barrymore's *Trial by Battle*. As was the convention for melodramas, the characters were rendered as stereotypes. To distance the script from the Thornton case, which had not yet been completed, and to make sure the legal authorities did not view it as contempt of court, Barrymore shifted the action from England to an unspecified European country and a world of castles and gothic interiors. The era was vaguely medieval. Abraham Thornton was now Baron Falconbridge, a ruthless and lustful villain; his victim Mary Ashford became Geralda, a simple country girl; and her brother and champion William became the brave Hubert. Barrymore's play has a band of smugglers, hired by dastardly Baron Falconbridge, abducting Geralda, who has resisted the Baron's efforts at seduction. Her brother Hubert and her father try to protect her, but the Baron kills her father. One of the smugglers, Henrie, who had previously refused to take part in the plot, rescues Geralda while her brother pursues the Baron to his castle. After a trial, the Baron and Hubert agree to a combat but it is Henrie, acting as champion for Geralda's family, who kills the Baron. Where in real life due process failed to provide the cathartic ending the public craved—justice for Mary and death for Thornton—Barrymore's third act delivered all that the supporters of Mary Ashford had wished for. In the imaginations of the audience, if nowhere else, the world was put to rights.

Barrymore, an actor and prolific writer of melodramas, was previously theatre manager at the Royal Surrey and at Astley's Amphitheatre, a horse-circus near Westminster Bridge, and specialised in spectacular staging. During this period audiences lapped up entertainment that brought real-life dramatic events to the stage.

On the night of 11 May 1818, however, behind the scenes at the Royal Coburg, things were not going smoothly. As the audience filed into the building at 5.30pm Richard Henry Norman, who played the Clown in the harlequinade, gave them handbills on which he aired his grievance. At 6.30pm the orchestra struck up 'God Save the King' and the audience joined in. Mr Munro, a distinguished actor on loan from the Theatre Royal, Edinburgh, who was playing the part of Baron Falconbridge, stepped forward to welcome the audience and give the address. Then, just as the curtain was about to rise on *Trial by Battle*, Norman appeared on stage to speak to the audience in person. He had been billed to perform in the harlequinade at the Royal Coburg at exactly the same time as he had been contracted to appear at Covent Garden, he told them. For this reason, he had wanted to change the order of the billing with the harlequinade or pantomime to be performed first. As I cannot in any way improve on *The Morning Post*'s description of how things went after that, I offer it in full.[83]

> After a short pause Mr Munro came forward to speak on behalf of Mr Glossop. He was endeavouring but with little prospect of success to make himself heard when Mr Norman again presented himself to state that 'his Clown dress was withheld from him by Mr Glossop.' On this news being received, the uproar became greater than ever.
>
> Mr Munro retired: the curtain was drawn up, and an attempt was made to go through the first scene of the Melodrama; but the strong disapprobation expressed caused its Author, Mr W. Barrymore, to advance, in order to make a new appeal for *Trial by Battle* and Mr Glossop; he was assailed by a shower of orange peel; the small ornamental railing which surmounted the orchestra partition was torn down and thrown on the stage; two of the lamps in front of it were broken, and the most violent tumult convulsed every part of the house. Mr Norman from time to time came forward to announce that Mr Glossop still retained his dress. To this no answer was given; both parties seemed resolved not to yield...
>
> After many unsuccessful attempts to obtain silence, Mr Barrymore accomplished so much of his purpose as to make it understood that the Managers wished to treat the public with all possible respect, but had been of the opinion that to change the order of the pieces would be to commence with impropriety.
>
> Mr Norman now again made his appearance and offered to speak; but as silence could not be instantaneously procured, he conveyed his meaning to the spectators by a few pantomimic flourishes, which intimated that he had been reinstated in his wardrobe and was going to dress for the Pantomime.
>
> The audience were regaled with music and a comic song by Mr Stebbing in the course of the next half hour and at eight o'clock the performance

commenced. Mr Norman and Mr T. Blanchard were very amusing as the Clown and Pantaloon.

A great variety of good scenery and some pleasant tricks compensated the holiday folks for the disappointment at first experienced and the exertions of the principal performers were requited with liberal applause.

Whatever the play lacked in literary merit was more than compensated for by glamour and spectacle, and by the new music, scenery, dresses and decorations. Despite the kerfuffle, the 'scenes were throughout well executed, and the performances are passable. The house was crowded to excess, and the pieces met with a good reception.'[84] Riots in theatres, while not everyday occurrences, were not unknown, so perhaps everyone just took the strife in their stride.

After the performance, the audience exiting the building would have seen that additional lights had been installed in the surrounding roads, including the new road to Waterloo Bridge, and the theatre management had also laid on extra patrols to guard against muggers and thieves.

Barrymore's *Trial by Battle* ran initially for fifteen nights and was still being sporadically performed in provincial theatres as late as the 1860s. Debate about the guilt or innocence of Abraham Thornton continued for much longer.

The communard and anarchist LOUISE MICHEL IN LAMBETH

> Louise Michel, whose lectures in this country are at present attracting some attention, has paid a visit to Lambeth Workhouse, with the view of inspecting the provision made for the comfort of the aged and unfortunate poor.
>
> *South London Press,* 13 January 1883

MISS FRANCES LORD,[85] a newly-elected member of the Lambeth Board of Poor Law Guardians, along with 'several [unnamed] ladies', on Thursday 11 January 1883, escorted a tall, thin middle-aged Frenchwoman dressed entirely in black around the workhouse in Renfrew Road, Kennington in south London. Lord's softly spoken and polite guest asked many questions and made a few remarks on the provision for the poor in England compared to France, and afterwards returned to her friends in Fitzrovia. She was the famous socialist and anarchist Louise Michel.

Twelve years earlier, in March 1871, Michel had taken part in the insurrection that led to the establishment of the Paris Commune, ten weeks of socialist government established in defiance of the right-wing republic. After its terrible and bloody fall during which, she later admitted, she had set fire to buildings, Michel was

FIG.1 Louise Michel photographed by Eugène Appert in the yard at Chantiers prison after the fall of the Paris Commune (1871).
Courtesy of Musée Carnavalet, Paris

sentenced to hard labour in a penal colony. So, why did Frances Lord invite an insurrectionist, convict and avowed atheist to tour the workhouse?

LOUISE MICHEL WAS born out of wedlock in 1830 in Vroncourt-la-Côte, a tiny hamlet in the Haute Marne, about a hundred and seventy-five miles southwest of Paris. Her mother was a chambermaid for a well-off local family and her father most likely the son of the house. He had little to do with her but his parents contributed to her upbringing and paid for her education. As a young woman, she worked as a schoolteacher, first locally, and later in Paris, and from an early age she was attracted to radical ideas about society, women's rights and the education of children. By 1860 Michel had moved to Montmartre, a largely working-class district in the north of Paris, where she opened a school which she ran on her own principles, by which children learned through play and discovery, and without the influence of the Catholic Church. During the 1870 Siege of Paris, when the city was cut off from the outside world by thirty thousand Prussian troops camped outside its walls, she ran the vigilance committee for Montmartre, her responsibilities including the provision of first aid to the National Guard defending Paris and requisitioning and redistributing food to those in need—Paris by then had begun to starve. She joined the National Guard herself and wore its uniform, a highly unusual move for a woman, and she was active in political clubs, where radical ideas were discussed.

Michel participated in the famous stand-off on 18 March 1871 between the army and the people of Montmartre. Government troops had attempted surreptitiously to remove two hundred cannon stored on the hill and Michel was among those who had rushed to the hill to confront them. The events of that day led directly to the establishment of the Commune and the subsequent (second) siege of Paris. During the downfall of the Commune at the end of May, often called the Bloody Week (*La Semaine Sanglante*), Michel was on active duty with the National Guard and led the defence of the barricade at Clignancourt and fought in the Père Lachaise cemetery. Afterwards, at a court martial, she was charged with trying to overthrow the government, encouraging citizens to arm themselves, using weapons and wearing a military uniform. She remained utterly unrepentant, admitted all the charges and requested

FIG.2 Louise Michel was persecuted by the French state. This portrait shows her at her trial in 1882. *Oil on canvas. Courtesy of Musée Carnavalet, Paris*

FIG.3 The last remaining building of Lambeth Workhouse, situated near Elephant and Castle, is now the home of the Cinema Museum. The workhouse was opened in 1874 and extended over almost eight acres. *Photo courtesy of Tim Clifford*

the death penalty. Instead she was given a sentence of hard labour for life in the French penal colony in New Caledonia in Polynesia.

When the French government granted a general amnesty to Communards in 1880 Michel was released and made her way back to France, stopping off in London. It was the start of a growing affection for the city. Although Britain was a monarchy and had an empire, forms of administration she detested, she was impressed by its strong tradition of political asylum—there were no immigration restrictions and refugees could not be extradited for political crimes. As she wrote in her memoirs:

> London! I love London, where my exiled friends have always been welcomed, London, where old England, standing in the shadow of the gallows, is still more liberal than the French bourgeois republicans are.[86]

In July 1881 Michel was back in London to attend the Anarchist Congress. The British press was deeply hostile. 'Her countenance is full of hate and discontent,' reported *The Dublin Evening Telegraph* whose 'Lady Correspondent' had been sent to a public meeting at Cleveland Hall to observe her:[87] 'Her fingers work in a nervous, agitated manner, and her whole frame is evidently under the influence of internal excitement. She was attired in black, with a cutthroat-looking bow of scarlet ribbon beneath her chin.'[88]

The Graphic reported that 'Mdlle. Louise Michel announced a second Golden Age, and counselled her hearers "not to spare their blood in bringing it about"'[89] but dismissed the ideas under discussion as unlikely to gain a foothold in Britain. In late 1882 *The World* labelled her 'slightly mad about the revolution' and described her rooms in the Boulevard Ornano in Paris as full of 'gloom and discomfort', littered with books, showing 'the scholar's carelessness doubled with the unthrift of poverty'; her clothes were shabby and she was 'dreadfully unkempt'.[90]

MICHEL RETURNED TO London on Sunday 7 January 1883, for a week-long series of twelve lectures at Steinway Hall in Lower Seymour Street.[91] This time, she was promoting specific causes: education, women's rights and social justice.

What prompted Miss Lord to invite Michel to see Lambeth Workhouse?[92] Perhaps she had become aware that Michel would be taking women's education rather than the violent overthrow of governments as her theme, and that she would also be raising money to fund a shelter for Communards in London who had fallen on hard times. We can speculate that for her part Michel accepted the invitation because she wanted to see how a workhouse with a particular reputation for humanity operated.

Lambeth Workhouse had not always had a good name. In January 1866 journalist James Greenwood of *The Pall Mall Gazette* went undercover in the old Lambeth workhouse in Princes Road. His report, 'A Night in a Workhouse',[93] exposed appalling conditions. He described inhumane overcrowding (thirty men in a room under ten metres square), bloodstained beds and 'mutton broth' baths. It is likely that if Michel had visited some years earlier her reaction would have been closer to that of Jules Vallès, a French journalist and left-wing political activist who escaped the bloodshed at the end of the Commune by fleeing to London. Vallès hated living in London and was highly critical of the political structures that maintained what he saw as a corrupt and rotten system. In his opinion, the workhouse was purgatory on earth, worse than Dante's *Inferno*. He spoke from experience, having been an inmate at one of the poorhouses in central London (he does not specify which) and described a heartless regime designed to keep people just alive but not much more, in which inmates were forced to do pointless labour and families were separated. In return for a place to sleep and a hunk of bread everyone had to do hard labour, '*les forts et … les faibles*' [the strong or the weak].[94]

Lambeth's new workhouse complex in Renfrew Road, finished in 1875 at a cost of £42,000, was designed to hold eight hundred and twenty inmates, and included dining halls, workshops, a bakehouse, as well as a corn-mill, laundry and engine room. The buildings were heated by open fires and were well ventilated.

The British press was noticeably warmer towards Michel during her 1883 visit than previously. The conservative publication *The St James's Gazette*, expecting a rough political firebrand, reported instead that she was a 'quiet, unpretentious, and well-mannered' woman who advocated, quite reasonably in their opinion, for women's education to

FIG.4　The entrance to a London workhouse. *A. Lanson, published in Jules Vallès'
La Rue à Londres (1884). Paris: G. Charpentier*

be put on an equal footing as men's so that they could earn money and keep themselves.[95]

On the day of the visit, Thursday 11 January 1883, Louise Michel left Fitzrovia and headed to Waterloo to be met by Miss Lord and her colleagues. They stopped first at the Old Vic in Waterloo, whose fortunes had recently been revived by social entrepreneur Emma Cons, who used it to provide education and cheap performances to working people. Michel and Lord afterwards walked on to Surrey Lodge in Kennington Road, which Cons had helped establish four years earlier as a new way to offer social housing, to meet Cons herself and take a look around.

Frances Lord wrote about the visit to Surrey Lodge for the *Westminster Gazette*:

> She [Miss Cons] told us of their history, their balance-sheet, and their success. Fire-proof walls, coal-box, side-board; as to sports, balconies for play; public wash-house, roofs for drying ground, public meeting room, and, above all, the great central garden for children to romp about in, all told Mdlle. Michel that whoever had thought about all this must be somebody who had worked among the poor for years, and resolved that sooner or later they should have this good thing, at rent within their means, if intelligence and love could give it them.[96]

The women walked on to Lambeth Workhouse in Renfrew Road (*Fig.3*). Here they stood in the Relief Hall while the 'poor people' filed in for a free meal. Michel inspected the Relieving Officer's book and Lord told her about his duties, which included visiting every new case of destitution to explain that no money would be paid out until the children went to school, and that the Board would cover the school fees. They chatted as they toured the corridors.

'Then no man or woman need starve in England,' remarked Michel.

'Nobody is to starve,' replied Miss Lord. 'But sometimes the poor people do not know where to apply, and in some parishes the food is bad, the relieving officers are careless and so on.'

'Yes, of course there will be mistakes, but still there is a meal here for all and a shelter for old age,' said Michel. 'Your government is very intelligent to let you all take your part in the work of public institutions, I do not wonder you all love your monarchy and do not wish to change it.'

'I think we are always changing it a very little, but we never knock things down violently, we try to prepare for change. This is the way we women have gradually come to take our modest share in public duty. First we got ready and then we began, it's no use to start till you're ready, is it?'

Michel admired some funeral wreaths laid out on a table and Lord told her that the daughter of a former Guardian who was 'always so fond of the poor people in the workhouse and came to see them often' had sent them in.

'Was it not good of her to think of them in all her trouble?' said Michel, adding, 'I understand England.'

That afternoon, Frances Lord accompanied Louise Michel to her next lecture at Steinway Hall. 'She said... that those wreaths and the public garden for the children's play in Surrey Lodge had thrown more light than anything she had ever seen before on the good forces that are always at work in our free country,' said Lord. That evening, she and Michel dined with the Reverend John Llewlyn Davies, a theologian and Anglican priest active in Christian socialist groups.[97] Reporting on the visit two days later, the *South London Press* crowed that 'Her visit to Lambeth seems to have inspired her with the idea that in Poor-law matters, they do not "do these things better in France."'[98]

On Monday 15 January Michel was back in Paris and continuing her life as a political activist and writer. Two days later, in London, at a scheduled meeting of the Lambeth Board of Guardians, members expressed surprise that Miss Lord had been happy to associate with 'a woman of extreme views'. 'No doubt she [Michel] had uttered many foolish things,' said Miss Lord in defence of her decision. 'But still, like others, the reports of her were exaggerated.'[99] Despite the personal criticism, Frances Lord had ensured that the work of the Lambeth Guardians had gained useful publicity. It had been framed as humanitarian and respectful by one of the most severe social commentators of the day.

In France, Michel continued to be harassed by the government and followed by police spies. Two months after her visit to London, in March 1883, she led a demonstration in Paris of unemployed workers during which she encouraged them to loot bakeries, for which she was sentenced to six years in solitary confinement. She served only three and used the time to write her memoirs. They contain reminiscences of the day she spent with Frances Lord in Lambeth.

She wrote she had been misunderstood on the subject of workhouses. Her hosts had thought she was enthusiastic about them, but that was not the case. 'I only stated the pleasure I felt over England's considering it a duty to be concerned about people who have neither food nor shelter. The thing that struck me—and I immediately said so—was the care with which in some workhouses, Lambeth for example, they soften the refuge where old Albion piles its poverty.'[100] The Lambeth Board of Guardians were certainly on the right track in terms of kindness and humanity, but for Michel, 'the green branches on the old tree cannot rejuvenate the rotten trunk'. She thought a social revolution would certainly take place in Britain, but because there was the outward appearance of care for the poor, it would take longer than elsewhere in Europe.

AFTER YEARS OF persecution by the French authorities, during which she was imprisoned and forcibly committed to a mental hospital, in 1890 Louise Michel returned to London, where for the final fifteen years of her life she lived semi-permanently. Soon after she arrived, Michel and other exiles established a school in Windmill Street for the children of anarchists.[101] This last phase of her life was highly productive. She frequently appeared at radical and socialist rallies and poured out articles, memoirs and poetry. Initially she lived in Fitzrovia, where French exiles tended to cluster, moving to south London in about 1894, living first in East Dulwich and later in Sydenham and Streatham. She was a popular speaker on both sides of the channel and her name continued to have major pulling power at radical and socialist meetings. She regularly returned to France to give speaking tours and it was on one of these that she fell ill, dying in Marseilles of pneumonia at the age of seventy-five. She was buried in the Levallois-Perret cemetery in Paris. Her funeral was attended by one hundred thousand people.[102]

NOTES

'I AM MURDERED': THE DEATH OF ELIZA FENNING

1. Old Bailey Proceedings Online (oldbaileyonline.org, version 8.0, 27 Jun. 2021), Apr. 1806, trial of Henry William Wyatt (t18060416-63).
2. The account of Eliza Fenning's case has been taken from multiple sources including *Globe*, 25, 27 Mar. 1815; *Morning Chronicle*, 18 May 1815; *Sussex Advertiser*, 7 Feb. 1825; *Independent Whig*, 22 Oct. 1815.
3. Anon. and Eliza Fenning (1815), *The case of Eliza Fenning who was convicted of attempting to poison the family of Mr. Turner by mixing arsenic in yeast dumplings: containing her trial, and the particulars of her execution, including... several affecting letters written a short time previous to her execution*. London: John Fairburn.
4. Charles Dickens (1836). *Sketches by Boz*. London: John McCrone.
5. Anon. (1846). Mr Adolphus and His Contemporaries at the Old Bailey, *Law Magazine*, Vol. 35, pp.54–67
6. Ben Wilson (2005), *The Laughter of Triumph*. London: Faber and Faber.
7. Hoods were to shield the observers from the gruesome sight of eyes protruding.
8. J. Watkins (1815), *The Important Results of an Elaborate Investigation into the Mysterious Case of Elizabeth Fenning*. London: William Hone.
9. J. Marshall (1815), *Five Cases of Recovery from the Effects of Arsenic with the Methods so Successfully Employed for Detecting the White Metallic Oxide ... relative to the guilt of Eliza Fenning*. London: C. Chapple.
10. *Public Ledger and Daily Advertiser*, 8 Apr. 1816.
11. William Hone (1816), *The Important Trials at Kingston, 5th April 1816*. London: W. Hone.
12. William Hone (1815), *La Pie Voleuse. The Narrative of the Magpie; or the Maid of Palaiseau. Being the History of the Maid and the Magpie. Founded upon the Circumstance of an Unfortunate Female having been Unjustly Sentenced to Death on Strong Presumptive Evidence*. London: J. Swan.
13. Walter Thornbury (1867), Old Stories Re-Told: Eliza Fenning (The Danger of Condemning to Death on Circumstantial Evidence Alone). *All the Year Round*, Vol. 18, No. 429, pp.66–72.

LOVE & LIES IN THE AGE OF ELOPEMENT

14. A longer exploration of the abduction of this intriguing and significant case can be found in my book *The Disappearance of Maria Glenn* (2016), published by Pen and Sword.
15. See Lisa O'Connell (2001). Dislocating Literature: The Novel and the Gretna Green Romance, 1770–1850. *NOVEL: A Forum on Fiction*, Vol. 35, No. 1, pp.5–23.
16. Jane Austen (1998), *Love and Freindship [sic] and Other Writings*. Ed. Janet Todd. London: Phoenix, pp.5–11, 12–26.
17. *The trial of Richard Vining Perry, Esq. for the forcible abduction, or stealing of an heiress, from the boarding-school of Miss Mills, in the city of Bristol...* (1794). Bristol: (no publisher). Perry later took the name of Clementina's benefactor, becoming Richard Vining Perry Ogilvie, and left Britain for Jamaica and the plantations he now owned as a result of his marriage to Clementina. In 1817, he is recorded as the 'owner' of 147 enslaved people on his estate at St Mary's. Clementina died in 1813 in Bath. George H. Gibbs (1947), *Bristol Postscripts*. Bristol: St Stephen's Bristol Press; *Gentleman's Magazine* (1813), Jul.–Dec., p.403.

18. Gretna Green, Scotland, Marriage Registers, 1794–1895 (The Lang Collection of Gretna Green Marriages Records).
19. Canning died in America in 1773, having married the great-nephew of the Governor of Connecticut and produced five children. There was no deathbed confession and her whereabouts in January 1753 remain a mystery. It has been suggested that she absented herself in order to give birth or to undergo an abortion, or that she was pursuing an illicit affair or was pushed into sex work. John Treherne's *The Canning Enigma* (1989, London: Jonathan Cape) is recommended reading on Canning, as is Dan Cruickshank's *The Secret History of Georgian London* (2010, London: Random House).
20. John Mathew Gutch (1817), *Caraboo: A Narrative of a Singular Imposition, Practised by a Young Woman of the Name of Mary Willcocks, Alias Baker, Alias Bakerstendht*. London: Baldwin, Cradock and Joy.
21. Anon. (1827), *The Trial of Edward Gibbon Wakefield and Frances Wakefield, indicted with Edward Thevenot, a Servant, for Conspiracy and for the Abduction of Miss Ellen Turner*. London: John Murray. In later life, Edward Wakefield became active in prison reform. He played a role in the development of South Australia, Canada, and New Zealand. Ellen Turner died in childbirth at the age of 19. Wakefield did not remarry.
22. *London Standard*, 31 Mar. 1842.

MRS MEREDITH, THE PRISONERS' FRIEND

23. *The Alexandra Magazine*, whose aim was to reach a readership of women already working for a living, closed in 1856 after about a year of publication. See: Sheila Herstein (1993). The Langham Place Circle and Feminist Publications of the 1860s. *Victorian Periodicals Review*, Vol. 26, No. 1, pp.24–7.
24. In 1864, the social reformer Mary Carpenter's book *Our Convicts* (1864, London: Longman, Green, Longman, Roberts & Green) alerted the public to the appalling conditions for women prisoners at Brixton Prison.
25. E.C. Wines (1873). *Report on the International Penitentiary Congress*. Washington: Government Printing Office, p. 237–8.
26. After the 1853 Penal Servitude Act, only long-term transportation remained. The final transportations took place in 1868.
27. Russell House was at 2 Mitcham Lane. It closed in 1888 when the premises were taken over by a Roman Catholic mission to fallen women.
28. Nine Elms Station was originally a goods stop but had been renamed Queen's Station or the Royal Station in 1854 when it was converted for the use of the Royal family. It was demolished in 1878. The current Nine Elms station, a stop on the Northern Line extension, was opened in 2021.
29. This equates to about £18 per annum. £20 for a live-in domestic servant was considered a good wage.
30. *Lloyd's Weekly Newspaper*, 19 Apr. 1881.
31. W. G. Blaikie, The Princess Mary's Village, Addlestone; *The Sunday Magazine*, 1875, p.420.
32. National Archives: 1871 England Census; Class: RG10; Piece: 671; Folio: 73; Page: 17; GSU roll: 823327
33. *Op. cit., The Sunday Magazine*.
34. The establishment was named after Princess Mary Adelaide, Duchess of Teck.
35. *The Star*, 27 Apr. 1880.
36. *The Daily News*, 25 Jul. 1871.

37. *Banffshire Journal and General Advertiser*, 31 Dec. 1878.
38. *The Wesleyan-Methodist Magazine* (1883), Series 6, Vol. 7, pp.142–9.
39. Lucia Zedner (1991). Women, Crime, and Penal Responses: A Historical Account. *Crime and Justice*, Vol. 14, p.338.
40. *Op. cit., Daily News*.
41. Mrs Meredith (1881). *A Book About Criminals*. London: James Nisbet.
42. *Op. cit., Daily News*; based on the advertised auction of lots when the laundry closed we can speculate that the move was prompted by a need to mechanise and expand the laundry operation.
43. *Evening Standard*, 2 Mar. 1883; *Rugby Advertiser*, 27 Oct. 1880. In order to survive, the venue offered diverse entertainments including music concerts and bicycle races which led to problems with the licensing authorities.
44. Anne Beale (1891), Prison Missions, *Newbery House Magazine*, Vol. 4, pp.718–24.
45. *South London Chronicle, 1 Aug. 1885*.
46. Dr McCall moved the clinic to her own home a few doors away at 131 Clapham Road. It subsequently moved to Fentiman Road (exact location unknown), McCall's new address at 161 Clapham Road, and eventually Jeffreys Road, the location of the Annie McCall Hospital.
47. *Morning Post*, 18 Jun. 1900.
48. *Morning Post*, 20 Dec. 1901.
49. Acknowledging the scholarship of the following: Helen Johnston & David Cox (2020). Gender and Release from Imprisonment: Convict Licensing Systems in Mid- to Late Nineteenth-Century England. In: M. Van der Heijden, M. Pluskota, & S. Muurling, eds, *Women's Criminality in Europe, 1600–1914* (pp. 134–47). Cambridge: Cambridge University Press. doi:10.1017/9781108774543.007; Jo Turner, Helen Johnston, Helen and Helen Waldman (2015). Female Prisoners, Aftercare and Release: Residential Provision and Support in Late Nineteenth-Century England. *British Journal of Community Justice*, Vol. 3, No. 3, pp.35–49.

THE ABOLITION OF THE JURY OF MATRONS

50. *Dundee Courier*, 17 Jan. 1931.
51. Thomas R. Forbes (1988), A Jury of Matrons, *Medical History*, Vol. 32, pp.23–33.
52. Lucy Kirkwood (2020), *The Welkin*. London: Nick Hern Books.
53. Anon. (1811), *Extraordinary Life and Character of Mary Bateman, the Yorkshire Witch*. Leeds: Davies and Co, Stanhope Press. Bateman was not pregnant and was executed at York on 20 March 1809.
54. *The Legal Observer, Or, Journal of Jurisprudence* (May-Oct. 1836), Vol. 16, p.206.
55. It was applied to the description of the foetus in an Anglo-Saxon metrical charm.
56. William Blackstone (1765), *Commentaries*, Amendment IX, Vol. 1, pp.120–41.
57. John Ayrton Paris, John Samuel Martin Fonblanque (1823), *Medical Jurisprudence*, Vol. 3, p.141.
58. National Archives: HO 47/53/20.
59. *Kentish Gazette*, 8 Aug. 1781.
60. Anon. (1812). Trial & execution of John Lomas, and condemnation of Edith Morrey, for wilful murder (broadside).
61. *Kentish Gazette*, 24 Jan. 1804; *Bell's Weekly Messenger*, 12 Feb 1804. Ann Hurle was hanged on 8 February 1804.

62. *Essex Standard*, 30 Mar. 1833; *Bury and Norwich Post*, 27 Mar. 1833.
63. Frederick Augustus Carrington, Joseph Payne (1839), *Reports of Cases Argued and Ruled at Nisi Prius, in the Courts of King's Bench & Common Pleas, and on the Circuit: from the Sittings in Michaelmas Term, 1823, to [Easter Term, 4 Vict. 1841]*, Vol. 8, p.262. London and Dublin: S. Sweet & R. Milliken and Son.
64. *Staffordshire Advertiser*, 12 May 1838. See also note 53.
65. *Op. cit.*, Forbes, pp.29–30.
66. *Globe*, 17 Jan. 1872.
67. *Op. cit.*, Forbes, p.32.
68. Quoted in *New York Times*, 4 Aug. 1879.
69. *Cornishman*, 28 Jun. 1906; *Royal Cornwall Gazette*, 12 Jul. 1906.
70. *The Suffragette*, 19 Dec. 1913
71. *Sheffield Daily Telegraph*, 5 Sep. 1932.
72. https://www.bbc.co.uk/news/world-asia-35589505 [retrieved 7 Jun. 2022].
73. *The Chemist*, Mar. 1851. In 1852 Archer published *A Manual of the Collodion Photographic Process*. Collodion is a flammable, syrupy solution of nitrocellulose in ether and alcohol.

CARTES DE VISITE OF WORKING WOMEN

74. Richard Knight Causton (1843–1929) and Selina Mary Chambers (dates unknown).
75. Later, it was a popular destination for Oscar Wilde, who often visited with his friend and companion Bosie (Lord Alfred Bruce Douglas).
76. I was astonished to find out that Causton's printing business was based in the premises behind my house in Stockwell, in southwest London, an odd coincidence given that Mrs Meredith's laundry (*see pp.44–55*) was in exactly the same location. One of the housing blocks now occupying the site is named Causton House.
77. Ilford went into administration in 2004–5.

TRIAL BY BATTLE: THE OPENING NIGHT OF THE ROYAL COBURG

78. William Barrymore (1759–1830), originally Blewit, an English actor at Drury Lane and the Haymarket and father of the pantomime actor William Barrymore (d. 1845), and progenitor of the Hollywood Barrymore family.
79. Further details of the case, including new evidence about Thornton, can be found in my book *The Murder of Mary Ashford* (2018) published by Pen and Sword.
80. Serres' wife became deluded and claimed that she was the illegitimate daughter of the King's brother the Duke of Cumberland, leading to the loss of his royal patronage, treatment that looks somewhat unfair given the King's own mental health problems.
81. Thomas Allen (1826), *The History and Antiquities of the Parish of Lambeth, and the Archepiscopal Palace in the County of Surrey*. London: J. Nichols, pp.297–302.
82. *Gentleman's Magazine* (Jan.–Jun. 1818), Vol. 88, p.559.
83. *Morning Post*, 12 May 1818.
84. *Saint James's Chronicle*, 12 May 1818.

LOUISE MICHEL IN LAMBETH

85. Henrietta Frances Lord (1848–1923), then aged 34, was a feminist, suffragist and Lambeth Poor Law guardian with a strong social conscience. She had studied at Girton College, Cambridge, and at University College, London. She was a friend of the writer and anti-war campaigner Olive Schreiner, who admired her 1882 translation of Ibsen's *The Doll's House*. Ibsen's biographer later wrote that it was the playwright's radicalism that induced Frances Lord to translate his work, which might indicate the sympathies that drew her to Louise Michel.
86. Louise Michel, *The Red Virgin: Memoirs of Louise Michel* (2003), transl. and ed. Bullitt Lowry, Elizabeth Ellington Gunter. University of Alabama Press, p.149. *Mémoires de Louise Michel, écrits par elle-même* (1886). Paris: F. Roy, is available to read online in French at gallica.fr and in English at Google Books.
87. Cleveland Hall, at 54 Cleveland Street, Marylebone, was the centre of the British secularist movement. It is no longer standing.
88. *Dublin Evening Telegraph*, 29 Jul. 1881.
89. 23 Jul. 1881
90. Quoted in *Civil & Military Gazette* (Lahore), 22 Dec. 1882.
91. The premises, a showroom for pianos and concert hall, were opened in 1875 on what is now known as Wigmore Street.
92. We have no evidence on whether Lord extended the invitation or Michel suggested it herself. Michel was in high demand, so it is more likely that Lord invited her.
93. 12 Jan. 1866.
94. Jules Vallès (1884), *La Rue à Londres*. Paris: G. Charpentiers.
95. 10 Jan. 1883.
96. Frances Lord's account was reprinted in *The Englishwoman's Review of Social and Industrial Questions*, Vol. 14, p.91.
97. Llewlyn Davies was the father of the children who inspired J.M. Barrie's stories of Peter Pan.
98. 13 Jan. 1883.
99. *South London Press*, 20 Jan. 1883.
100. *Op. cit.*, Michel, *The Red Virgin*, p.148.
101. The school moved to Fitzroy Street and closed in 1892 after bombs were found in the basement, probably the work of a police spy who had taken a job as the school's assistant.
102. The classic French language biography of Louise Michel is *Louise Michel ou La Velléda de l'anarchie* by Edith Thomas (1971, Gaillard). It is published in an English translation by Black Rose Books (1980, Montréal). Paul Foot's remarkable 1979 lecture on Louise Michel is available on YouTube: youtu.be/IfQojkzsikE

ACKNOWLEDGEMENTS

My heartfelt thanks to designer Caroline Jefford and my partner Tim Clifford. As ever, the staff at the National Archives, the British Library and various collections around the country have been amazing.

CARET PRESS

Caret Press is an independent publishing imprint based in London and established in 2021. We specialise in history, essay collections and historical fiction.

Order our books from Amazon and bookshops. Ebook versions are on all major platforms.

To submit your own work for publication please contact us at info@caretpress. We accept completed manuscripts only.

Visit our website caretpress.com.

OTHER CARET PRESS PUBLICATIONS

Under Fire: The Blitz Diaries of a Volunteer Ambulance Driver (2021) by Naomi Clifford

Six Essays on Vauxhall Gardens (2021) by David E. Coke

The 1914 Diary of Dora Lourie by Naomi Clifford (in preparation)

These Were Our Sons: Stories from Stockwell War Memorial by Naomi Clifford and others (in preparation)

www.ingramcontent.com/pod-product-compliance
Lightning Source LLC
Chambersburg PA
CBHW051331110526
44590CB00032B/4481